MW01247716

WALKING IN THE WONDER

*A Memoir of Gratitude
for a Lifetime of Miracles*

Jannie Wright

AuthorHouse™
1663 Liberty Drive
Bloomington, IN 47403
www.authorhouse.com
Phone: 1-800-839-8640

© 2011 Janet A. Wright. All rights reserved.

No part of this book may be reproduced, stored in a retrieval system,
or transmitted by any means without the written permission of the author.

First published by AuthorHouse 6/23/2011

ISBN: 978-1-4567-5595-9 (sc)

Library of Congress Control Number: 2011907442

Printed in the United States of America
Certain stock imagery © Thinkstock.
This book is printed on acid-free paper.

authorHOUSE®

DEDICATED TO
Father/Mother Creator of All, light of my soul
Daughter Wendy Joy, light of my life
Carol Ann McKievick, light of my heart

WITH THANKS TO
Paul and Rena, my parents, who blessed their three
children with invaluable lessons born of love, honesty,
good humor and nurturing

AND TO
Grandson Jack, now age five. Since birth, you've
brightened our lives like a radiant burst of sunshine.
It will be fun to watch as you journey into the future,
enlightening the world wherever life leads you!

FOREWORD

I am so honored to have this opportunity to write the Foreword to Jannie Wright's *Walking in the Wonder*. It causes me to reflect on some of the most moving writing I have encountered. That is saying something because I majored in English Lit.

Jannie's words turn rapidly into emotional brilliance. I guarantee you a kaleidoscopic experience. The background is alight with love and bits of sparkling anecdotes re-arranging themselves into a constant display of bright emotional stories. Turn the page as you would twist a kaleidoscope, and you will discover a new and entrancing view of life.

You will laugh. You will sigh. You will cry. You will cry as you recall incidents in your own life. You will dig deeply into your own emotions, which may have been suppressed, to find yourself in tears but not in sorrow. Why? Because here you have found a soul who magically transports human experiences into print in a way that lets the reader feel like a participant in each gently unfolding journey.

Chaucer was a great story teller. Shakespeare was a consummate playwright. Emerson inspired us. Jannie draws up deep emotions many of us have repressed in our efforts to cope with life. In her own charming way, she manages to turn our feelings into an exuberant and majestic tribute to life itself.

Here you will meet a sincere and loving soul who shares with you a rainbow of inspiring true stories. Many of these are richly infused with what some call coincidence and others term "synchronicity." Carl Jung, the Swiss psychologist, discussed synchronicity at length, but deliberately decided not to give it a clear definition. To quote from Jung: "Causality is the way we explain the link between two successive events. Synchronicity designates the parallelism of time and meaning between psychic and psychophysical events which scientific knowledge so far has been unable to reduce to a common principle." Jannie, however, plunges right into the matter with many examples of unexplained coincidences. I leave it to the reader to decide whether Jannie's stories cause us to pause and consider more closely the parallelism, the synchronicity, of many events in our own lives.

You love her and *life* when you finish this remarkable book.
Frank L. McKibbin, author and columnist
September 25, 2010

ACKNOWLEDGMENTS

At first I tried to list everyone who helped bring this book into its final form, but when the number reached 150, it seemed silly to just tally name after name. There'd be pages and pages of them, with nothing to indicate what each one had done.

While searching for a solution, suddenly the light dawned. I realized, "What a delicious dilemma!" How wonderful to have so *many* special friends. It reminded me of a little plaque on my dining room wall that reads, "Count your blessings by smiles, not tears—Count your age by friends, not years."

The logical and fair thing to do is to list you all by categories. In trying to name each and every individual, I would inevitably leave someone out. Please search for yourself in the following descriptions. You will be able to spot precisely where *you* fit in:

To the steadfast people who have been present since my birth in 1945, the new friends encountered this past year, and the myriads who have come along throughout the times in between—I treasure you *all*.

To the men and women who have been like older brothers and sisters or mother and father figures, your counsel over the years has been much appreciated. You have shared generously your own life experiences, and it is an *honor* to know you.

To all my teachers, loads of gratitude for helping me learn how to express my thoughts clearly.

I am personally acquainted with several writers. You have each shared many of your own works, and let me learn from those unique literary efforts. Thank you for sharing personal experiences. It's a privilege to be able to call each of you *"friend."*

I owe a huge debt of gratitude to those of you who read and reviewed these writings, offering encouragement and suggestions ranging from grammar and punctuation to clarity of content. Because of you, this book has been able to reach its full potential. You all deserve *thanks beyond measure*.

If you are a creator of music, please know the special place music holds in my heart. Melodies and words have been my companions through the ups and downs and sideways turns of living…and loving. Thanks to *each* of you for following your own bliss, and taking all of us who love your creations along for the ride.

If we ever dated in years gone by, *thank you* for the valuable life lessons you taught me during the times we shared.

There are countless neighbors I wish to thank, for your smiles and laughter, and for the times we have helped one another. Thank you to the one constant neighbor who has been here over the span of many years. My front door faces your own about eight feet away. You are like the sister I never had. I'm grateful for all the shared conversations. Thank you now and always for our special and *enduring friendship*.

Many persons reading this book will discover themselves in the stories. If you are one, *thank you* for all you have meant in my life, for all *you* have contributed to these true tales.

There are six who *will* find your names accompanied by words of thanks in the DEDICATION. But mere words fall far short in describing the *gratitude* and *love* I feel for all of *you*.

Where would any of us be without the love and support of people who share our travels as we walk the sometimes gentle, sometimes rocky, yet always fascinating pathway of life? *THANK YOU, ONE AND ALL!*

Contents

I. LIFE'S JOYS AND MIRACLES (True Stories)

II. LYRICAL THOUGHTS (Poems)

III. LIFE'S LESSONS LEARNED (Essays)

INTRODUCTION

Congratulations to you for choosing to reach for this lovely book. Open to any page, and you will see the insight of my dear friend of 50 years. Go ahead—I'll wait right here for you....

Thanks for coming back. What did you think? I believe that Jannie sees significant messages connecting to her life as she lives that adventure each day. Not many of us can do that!

Often, in the stories that follow, when it seemed an adventure was *finished*, a place where most people might choose to stop, Jannie took one more step in kindness and outrageous hope... and then a miracle happened.

The 15-year-old girl I met at summer camp at Doane College in Crete, Nebraska 50 years ago, made an "instant connection" with me. We even share the same birthday. Although we came from very different areas (She lived in what I believed to be the BIG city of Omaha, and I came from a farm in the rural community of Seward), our identical view of life was extraordinary. Jannie shared her miracle stories with me over time, and she will do the same with you in the pages of *Walking in the Wonder*. Keep this book nearby. You will open it many times as your ultimate Power speaks to you, whatever you choose to call that Power.

Jannie has spent her life observing people, listening to them, and trying to understand what makes each one uniquely *who* they are. She is always optimistic. Everything in this book has a positive aspect to it. People are more alike than different. Yet, it is the unique talents and personal qualities of each individual that makes humankind so exciting to study—a rainbow of beauty and possibility. Jannie is ecumenical in her outlook, and appreciates truths found in a variety of different spiritual beliefs. She believes there is One Creator of us all, referred to by many names.

Every day and every moment is another new adventure for her. Things that seem trivial and everyday become events to be celebrated. Loss becomes just a temporary lapse in the grand scheme of our lives.

During my 40-year nursing career, I have witnessed my fellow humans passing to the other side. It can be awesome, comforting and very spiritual. Loved ones do return with messages to guide our steps when we stumble. Love is wisdom.

Every life has its mountaintop and valley experiences. When you finish *Walking in the Wonder*, you will feel you've been on a vacation in the Swiss Alps. Consider this book the diary of a friend who experienced some uncanny miracles of synchronicity, and with each said, "WOW! That's interesting!" She recorded many of them, and now shares them with you.

Whatever your own thoughts about life, feel free to pour yourself a soothing cup of tea, coffee or cocoa and settle in for a fun adventure. You will find a warm, cozy place to relax within these pages of *Walking in the Wonder*.

Judy Nagel, RN (Retired)
Former Director of Nursing, Long Term Care
Michigamme, MI

I. LIFE'S JOYS AND MIRACLES
(True Stories)

NO ONE IS ALONE

In the late 1960s, while in my early twenties, I lived in a bachelorette apartment in Pacific Beach on the coast of San Diego, California. Life was good. I had a nice job in banking, good friends, and lived in a beautiful resort city. I fancied myself living a life similar to Mary Richards, the main character on television's *The Mary Tyler Moore Show*…a carefree, single woman.

One night, while reading a novel at the apartment, suddenly a warmth came into my stomach. It traveled upward and eventually exited through my shoulders and the top of my head. I heard a male voice inside my mind say, "You will never be alone." I was left filled with a sort of euphoria, as if a huge boulder had been lifted from me. I felt very light and free, although, as I said in the beginning, I hadn't been feeling low or depressed in my current circumstances. Whatever this was, it filled me with great happiness. I laid the book down and wondered, "What is THIS?" I had not been thinking about spiritual things when it happened. Nevertheless, it was a *spiritual* happening. *Whose* voice was it? I still don't know.

Time passed. In the mid 1980s, I wrote a poem entitled "Street People." One of the recurring lines was "No one is alone." Soon after that poem was written, playwright Stephen Sondheim came to the Old Globe Theater in San Diego to write a new musical entitled *Into the Woods*. He had written the lyrics for *West Side Story*, and has since become the author/composer of many other musicals. Because I was hoping to turn some of my words into song lyrics, I gathered together a selection of poems and wrote a letter to Mr. Sondheim, leaving the entire package in his "mailbox" at the Old Globe. I explained that I realized he was very busy, but if he had an opportunity to do so, could he please let me know if he deemed any of the poems suitable enough to one day be put to music?

A short time passed. One Sunday night, while my daughter Wendy and I were watching the TV show *60 Minutes*, the phone rang. Wendy said, "Mom, it's some guy."

"Hi, Janet, it's Steve Sondheim."

"Sure," I said, thinking it was one of my male friends playing a joke.

"No, it really *IS*."

We talked for about half an hour. He related things that were going on with his new show. Eventually, we spoke of the poems. He explained to me that lyrics are a funny thing. Until the singer tries to actually sing them, it's hard to know if the pronunciation will come across effortlessly, how they will sound when combined with the music. He spoke to me of a certain quatrain I had written in the poem entitled "Street People." I didn't even know what a "quatrain" was, never having heard the word. "No one is alone" was part of that poem.

About two weeks later, an item appeared in our local newspaper's gossip column. Stephen Sondheim had added a new song to the third act entitled, *No One Is Alone*. I thought, "Oh my goodness, has he taken my poem and claimed it as his own work?" I called the house manager at the Old Globe and explained the situation. She invited me to come to the theater and peek in during the third act to listen to the lyrics of the new song. So Wendy and I did just that. It turned out he had only used the phrase "no one is alone." Then he built his own song around those four words.

Later, I read in a *TIME* magazine article that Mr. Sondheim would often take snatches of conversations he overheard, or little phrases he encountered, and then build songs around them.

English jazz artist Cleo Laine recorded *No One Is Alone*, which had become the hit tune of the show. It was nominated for a Grammy award. The musical found its way to Broadway and became a big success. I was watching *60 Minutes* on a subsequent Sunday evening when Diane Sawyer asked singer Bernadette Peters (a cast member of *Into the Woods*), "Is there one song that is quintessentially Sondheim?" Bernadette said, yes, there was one. It was called *No One Is Alone*. The little kid inside of me shouted, "But that's quintessentially ME!"

Oh, well. It was comforting to know that audiences both on Broadway and in other cities were being touched by the realization they were not alone. No one is alone.

More time passed. A tragedy happened in the world of figure skating. Sergei Grinkov, a young pairs skater from Russia, died of a heart attack while rehearsing with his wife and partner, Ekaterina Gordeeva. His death left her alone to raise their young daughter, the couple's pride and joy.

Soon, Scott Hamilton's ice show came to San Diego. My best friend Carol and I went to see it, securing seats halfway up with a good view of the entire arena. At one point in the show, the house went completely dark. A pin spot light was focused on the doorway where the skaters entered. There, skating into the arena, alone as a solo performer, came Ekaterina Gordeeva. She was floating across the ice to the song *No One Is Alone*. Carol leaned over, smiled and whispered, "What if you had never written the original poem?"

Fast forward to 2004. I was watching the TV show *Crossing Over with John Edward*. He is a gifted medium who brings through people's relatives who have passed away. At one point in the show, he told a woman in the audience that her father was there in spirit and wished to express to her over and over that "You are not alone." The woman began to cry. She explained that years earlier she had been a singer performing in the musical *Into the Woods*. Her father and the rest of the family had not spoken to her for years. But he came to hear her sing. He was impressed by the song, and was moved so much that he came backstage. They had a reconciliation, and told each other that neither of them need ever be alone again. She was able to enjoy some years with her dad before he passed away.

I ask myself, when is this story going to end? If that family was affected by those words, perhaps many others of the thousands who have seen and will see the show might have their hearts touched as well.

So I wish to say thank you: To *Whomever* it was that came to my soul in my twenties and made me feel so good; and to whatever creative Force initiated the inspiration that aided in writing the poem. It just seemed to flow onto the paper without much thought. Finally, *thank you* to Stephen Sondheim, for creatively sowing the seeds of those four words, and proliferating their message around the world. Truly, no one is alone.

Bachelorette days, age 25, wearing bank "uniform"

THE MUSIC LIBRARY

In December of 1997, my loved one, Carol McKievick, was diagnosed with Stage IV terminal ovarian cancer. From that time until late spring, we shared my apartment so I could look after her 24/7. In mid-April, we moved into the San Diego Hospice, living there together until her passing May 9, 1998.

One evening, we were playing a CD of beautiful flute music by James Galway. Melodies drifted across the expansive hallway into the opposite room occupied by a patient named Dorothy. The following morning, after Dorothy had passed away, her nurse shared this story with us: Dorothy had no family or friends there during her final hours. When she heard our music, she remarked to the nurse, "Oh, that is so beautiful. I wish I had music in MY room."

After Carol's own passing, I began thinking about a fitting memorial for her. She had been the first chair French horn player in a symphony orchestra. I remembered Dorothy's wish. Thus was begun the Music Library at the San Diego Hospice, dedicated in Carol's name. Each of the 24 rooms received a CD/Cassette/AM-FM player. The library began with 100 CDs. By the year 2000, there were hundreds more, thanks to donations from grateful family members of patients who had been comforted by the library's CDs. The expanded library consisted of many different types of music, in various languages, including even lullabies for the youngest of patients.

In late January of 2000, I again moved into the hospice to live with my father, Paul Wright, who was passing away from Alzheimer's. Having learned of the increased number of CDs, I asked a nurse if I might see the room where all of these were kept. She graciously offered, "Sure, follow me." We entered a small room with some file cabinets, the kind with four drawers, each about four feet across. She reached down to the third drawer of one of the cabinets and pulled it open. There, stored on their edges, were two long rows of CDs. My eyes fell upon one entitled, *Solo Harp.* I remarked to the nurse, "I'll bet my Dad would like this one." I removed it and we left, having been in the room only about a minute and a half.

Over the course of the next three days, we played that CD along with others brought from home. Because it was an instrumental, I didn't bother to notice the title of each selection. On the morning of the third day, I wondered, "What are the titles of the pieces on that harp CD?"

Before revealing the answer, I must share that when my brother Will was young, Dad's nickname for him was Terwilliger. Will would come into the room and Dad would say, "Hi, Terwilliger!" Also, having spent some time working in a hardware store in his younger years, he would often tell us about funny names for machinery parts; one example being "widget."

As I picked up the CD, I was stunned to see that one of the songs was entitled, *Terwilliger-Widget*. Just below that title was listed another song, *William's Lullaby*.

Why did the nurse open the third drawer of that particular cabinet? What made my eyes fall upon that one particular CD? Finally, how many CDs in the known universe include a song entitled, *Terwilliger-Widget*? What did it all mean? I like to think Carol was saying, "I love my music library."

Thank you, Carol, for your life and your courageous battle with cancer. Because you were in residence at the hospice, the idea was born to bring music to thousands of patients who have come after you. Of course, *ultimate* thanks belong to Dorothy, for making her wishes known.

For ten years, I was a volunteer baby "cuddler" at a large hospital here in San Diego. They, too, adopted the CD library idea after observing the program at the hospice. The nurse's station on each floor has players and CDs to lend to patients. There are even audio books on CDs. Thousands through the generations will benefit from Carol's music. Hers is a *living* memorial. As affirmed in print on the side of each CD player at the hospice, "Her music never ends."

Related writings: "HONORING CAROL," "IN THE COOL MIST OF YOSEMITE," "THE LOVE OF MY FATHER," "DAD AND HIS THREES," "A GLIMPSE OF HEAVEN," and "SUZE ORMAN."

HONORING THE TINIEST AMONG US

For several years, I've been privileged to spend a few hours one evening each week as a volunteer in a hospital neonatal intensive care unit (NICU) in San Diego. Those of us who do this work have the job title "Cuddler" on our identification badges. Having been in the business world for over thirty years in a salaried capacity, I can honestly say this is the most "rewarding" work ever in my lifetime.

Many years ago, in the *San Diego Union Tribune,* there appeared a feature article (with full color pictures) about two volunteers working with newborns in the NICU. Both were men about 65 years old. Learning how blessed they felt about this volunteer "job" inspired me to sign up on the waiting list.

Two years later, the hospital called to ask if I was still interested. Evidently, this is a *very* popular avocation, given the number of people that apply. I now understand WHY.

Imagine walking into a nursery where the infants are only one, two or three pounds. A nurse hails you from the other side of the room, "I'm so glad you're here! This little one has been crying off and on for hours and really needs to be cuddled." You pick up the infant and settle into the rocking glider chair provided. Resting the baby's head just over your heart, you gently begin to rock, softly humming. The little one seems to notice something is different. He or she looks in the direction of the melodic humming. Within less than a minute, relaxation takes over. A face that had been deeply flushed red and purple from crying returns to a soft pink or tan or brown. Shortly thereafter, the baby's eyes softly close.

It is a moment that makes one feel so *useful* in the scheme of life. These little ones give all of us who work in the NICU such special gifts. The reciprocal give and take of a tender loving touch is one example. Hearing a soft comforting voice reassures and relaxes them. The warmth of these moments is special to both babies and cuddlers.

On one occasion, a little girl kept looking up at the ceiling. Her eyes were darting to and fro as if she were watching butterflies flit here and there. One of the head nurses has a special gift of "seeing" spirit. I asked him what he thought she was looking at, because to my eyes it was just a white ceiling. He suggested, "Well, she has just come from heaven. She probably still sees angels all around."

From what I have read, heaven is filled with beautiful music. Perhaps that is why the babies respond to humming. They are remembering music as opposed to the cacophony of chatter in the nursery. Attending nurses don't hold back or try to whisper. These babies go directly from the dark quiet comfort of the womb into bright lights and normally pitched voices. Lots of voices. Blankets are placed over the top third portion of open cribs to shield newborns' eyes. Quilts are positioned over the sealed incubators to help block out bright lights, making it easier for the babies to rest. A child born healthy with no complications is usually kept in its mother's room. The nursery typically houses sick children born either with abnormalities or very prematurely.

Multiple births are enchanting to see in the intensive care unit. The twins, triplets or quadruplets are placed together in the same crib. Picture it: in the case of triplets, three little ones spooning each other, lying side by side in the same direction, each with a little arm draped over the baby next to it in a soft hug. It's one of the cutest things I've ever seen. Babies are positioned in such fashion because they have become used to each other in utero. Remaining close after birth helps them to thrive.

Take a moment to imagine what a baby undergoes at birth—being born into a world where no one explains why certain things are being done to you. There are surgeries both inside the womb and after babies are born. There are eye exams and insertions of intravenous needles into the back of a baby's hand or the top of its foot. Some children are born with their intestines outside the body and must undergo surgery right away to put things in their proper place. These little ones must wonder (in perplexing thoughts and feelings of their own), "Why are these people poking me and doing these things?" They are vocal in letting us know when they're in pain. One thing I consider a blessing: these tiny ones seem to live in the moment, with no concept of future. Once the pain ends and they are held and comforted, they usually settle right down.

Babies over these many years have taught me certain things. Most will settle down and stop crying if they are swaddled tightly in a blanket (so their arms don't flail around), then rocked gently with humming. Binkies (pacifiers) are a great comforter for many. Sometimes a baby is just too warm and wants NO blanket. I will never forget one little boy who would only settle down and go to sleep if you bounced him on your knee (gently, of course).

Feeding time is special. There are lots of ways these little ones choose to enjoy mealtime if they don't have the blessing of a nursing mother. Some are big eaters who know exactly what to do with a bottle's nipple. Others are very slow to take to it as we try to coax them into a delicious repast. A few even need help moving their jaws up and down for suction, guided by one of our fingers placed under their chins for support. Some are fed via a tube to the stomach, but still love to have their cuddling time.

Less fortunate children are born addicted to drugs, and need to be brought down slowly from that dependence. These little ones have a very distinctive high-pitched squeal and will often tremble. Some of the mothers literally deliver a baby, then walk out of the hospital to get their next illicit drug fix, and never look back. Many of these children are placed in foster care.

Most stories have happy endings with babies going home. Once in a while, things do not turn out so well. I remember one little boy who had an illness not seen before for which there was no known cure or treatment. Doctors and nurses were just trying to keep him comfortable until he could be moved into hospice care. Holding him made me realize what a very *holy* place the nursery is. If what I have read is true, that we choose how we come to earth and literally choose our parents, these are very courageous souls indeed. What a difficult time just now to enter the earth experience. The future is so uncertain and problems are many. I feel honored to be in the presence of these very special little ones.

If we have any kind of communicable illness, we are, for obvious reasons, advised not to go to our shift. Once I was off for about three weeks. It made me realize how special these hours in the nursery are. I thought, "If someday someone says I can no longer do this work, how very empty this one night a week will seem." Thank you to the hospital, the nurses, and most especially these tiny ones for letting me share in their lives. It is a spectacular privilege and great honor to be part of such a beautiful and caring environment.

(Confidentiality is very much a part of our training. We are advised not to share names or other details, which is why I have left out the name of the hospital and all other identifying information. If this sounds like an interesting opportunity, check with your local hospital. Many have "cuddler" programs and would love to interview new applicants.)

Related writing: "AND A LITTLE CHILD SHALL LEAD THEM."

THE LOVE OF MY FATHER

Most people are familiar with the old axiom regarding the bond between fathers and daughters, and the one between mothers and sons. I had a wonderful mother, but this piece will be all about my dad. How fortunate I've been as a child, young woman, and one who has reached maturity, to have had such a unique man in my life.

Paul Milton Wright (his middle name honored English poet John Milton) was born March 30, 1910. As a teenager, he quit school to help the family when his own father passed away. Dad was a self-taught, eager learner who loved to read, and later became a wonderful writer. When young, he worked in an auto parts store and labored briefly as a mechanic. During the Great Depression, Dad gave driving lessons in his own car. "And I had to pay for the gas!" He later found a mentor in insurance, opened his own agency, and traveled Nebraska as a salesman, recruiting other agents along the way.

Dad had the gentlest of hearts. As a young boy, he watched broken hearted as a truck ran over his little dog right in front of him. He was so distraught, he vowed never to own another one. He never did. Animals always took to Dad. I loved watching him put bits of food into the palm of his hand. Backyard birds flew to land on the edge of his palm and hungrily accept the morsels. He had great respect for all of life. Dad would catch a fly in the house, hold his closed hand up to my ear so I could hear it buzzing, then open the door and release it into the fresh air. I felt he instinctively knew all creatures on earth need to be respected for the unique lives they lead and the challenges they face. Dad gave the same gentle care to the plants in his yard. He was a brilliant thinker. I often wondered, during his quiet time of tending to nature, what might have been the subjects of his thoughts. He seemed knowledgeable in so many different areas.

Dad changed careers, leaving insurance for the real estate profession. He became the number one real estate agent in Omaha, Nebraska. I remember one month when he sold seven homes. Mom said that was his most spectacular month ever. Dad was known for his business ethics. His word was his bond. He took great care in matching people to the home that was just right for them. As a result, when folks were ready to move on to their next home, they would look him up once again. On one occasion, because of his fine reputation, when he changed agencies, the new firm took out an ad in the Omaha newspaper. All it said was, "Paul Wright now works for.........."

Dad didn't shout or use profanity, and neither did my mother. We had a peaceful home in which there were moments of laughter and lots of smiles. Dad was home every night for dinner.

I remember the five of us gathered around at suppertime; Mom, Dad, my two older brothers, Bob and Will, and me. There were conversations about what was going on in our lives. At the end of the meal, Dad would often pile the dishes up in front of him, gather all the glasses, and pick up his spoon to play spur-of-the-moment "tunes" for us. We would giggle and Mom, placing dessert on the table, would softly ask, "How do you expect them to learn any MANNERS when you do these crazy things?" Dad loved his desserts, and sometimes would have two. Yet during his whole adult life, he seemed to stay within five pounds of the same steady weight. I so envied him that.

Yes, our dad was a funny man. He used to pretend to be television comedian Jackie Gleason, dancing around the living room and doing impressions of Jackie's characters. He created so many funny moments. In the evenings we would watch light-hearted shows like "Jack Benny," "Bob Hope," "Milton Berle," "Sid Caesar," and "Ed Sullivan's Toast of the Town." Dad cooked popcorn to accompany our TV viewing, dividing it into little individual bowls. The large bowl remained in his lap, a privilege reserved for the head of the family.

He was raised a Christian Scientist, and a couple of times during his life hovered near death. But he just asked to be left alone, promising that he and God would take care of restoring him back to health. True to his word, he did recover. Dad once remarked to me when I was in my thirties, "People nowadays are too impatient for healing. If you give the body nutritionally what it needs, pray and have some patience, the body will heal itself." He believed in having broken bones put in place. He did go to the dentist to have cavities filled, but didn't use novocaine (ouch!). He lived until just two months shy of his 90th birthday.

One of Dad's greatest talents was as a profitable investor in the stock market. During my working years, whenever I had saved a little extra money and asked for advice, he would choose a stock for me. I never lost money with any of those investments. He usually would be doing exactly the opposite of what the big houses like Merrill Lynch were advising. Yet he was very successful. Family friends would ask his advice about how to invest their money. He had talents in so many areas. That was our dad.

He and Mom met on a public golf course. Later, Dad became quite proficient in the game, and we have a newspaper photo of him in a pair of knickers, taking a swing in the Western Amateur competition. All three of his children learned to play golf while we were growing up. It's a wonderful sport, providing exercise in the beauty of nature and lessons in self-discipline: how to control one's anger after a bad shot, contrasted with the sheer joy of hitting an amazing one. The ups and downs of golf provide many good lessons for life itself.

In my youth, I thought Dad resembled Clark Gable, mustache and all (yet even more good-looking). We attended a father-daughter dinner dance when I was a Campfire Girl. I thought him the handsomest man in the room. We shared a waltz, and I was so proud to be his partner.

When the chips were down, Dad was there. Having filed for an annulment after seven years of marriage, losing our home, and realizing I would now be a single mother with a small child to raise, I sat in his kitchen and told him I felt like I was going to pieces. The future was filled with so much uncertainty and responsibility. I didn't know where I would find a lucrative career, where we would live, or how I could give my daughter Wendy a middle class upbringing. Dad reached over, took hold of my hand and said, "As much as anyone in this world loves anyone else, that's how much I love you. You can either let this situation defeat you, or you can get up and move forward with the best you can give. There are only two choices and there is no middle ground." Three sentences, yet I remember them to this day.

Dad was very wise. Everything turned out fine. We were able to live the life I had envisioned for us. It would have been easy for him to just give us money. But that would be a temporary stopgap solution. As the old saying goes, "Give a man a fish and he will eat for a day. Teach him how to fish and he will eat for a lifetime."

My father retired in 1962 at fifty-two years of age. In his early eighties, we noticed his memory beginning to fail. He was in the first stages of Alzheimer's. We didn't mention that word around him. One day, while sitting alone with me in his living room, he looked into my eyes and asked for a promise: "Never forget how much I love you." To me, it meant he realized he was forgetting things. He must have thought it important to provide a solid assurance of the extent of his love.

As time progressed, Mom became exhausted caring for Dad. It seemed if something were not done to help her, she might pass away from the sheer stress of their situation. Luckily, on a hilltop halfway between Mom's house and my apartment, a special facility solely for the care of Alzheimer's patients was being completed. My brother Will and his lady love Dorothea flew in from Florida and furnished one of the rooms beautifully, complete with photos of Dad's mother and father atop the chest of drawers.

The scene was set. Mom asked Dad if he would like to go with her to a new senior center for a free lunch. He said sure, and I drove the three of us to a beautiful new place, complete with a central skylight and open doors so patients could roam freely both indoors and out in the fresh air. The outdoor walkways and gardens were tastefully protected with a tall brick wall surrounding the entire property.

Upon entering the lobby, the three of us were greeted and offered the chance to view one of the rooms. We ushered Dad into the room specially decorated just for him. "Look!" he exclaimed, "There's a picture of my mother and one of my dad!" He had a huge grin on his face. After a few minutes, we went to the dining room where the chef had prepared a delicious lunch. Halfway through the meal, Mom leaned over and whispered, "I want you to be the one to tell him he has to stay here when we go home." I remember panicking, wondering how I could tell Dad, this kind and gentle man, something of such great import without breaking his heart.

I'm sure Divine Guidance came into play. When we had finished eating, I mentioned to Dad how difficult it was for Mom to cook for him and do laundry; especially since lately she was having so much pain in her leg. I reminded him that everything at this new senior center was free. "Would you be willing to stay here for a little while until Mom's leg gets better?" He thought for a moment, nodded, and said, "Okay. Do you think I could stay in that room with the pictures of my mom and dad?" He didn't even think it "unusual" that someplace not his home would have pictures of his parents in it. Not a tear. No hesitation. Dad lived there for several years. I never saw him cry. Yes, Alzheimer's is an awful illness, but in some ways it seems to protect the heart and feelings. Dad was a financial genius. But later, when I asked if he could add the numbers twelve and three, he thought a moment and replied, "Hmmm. Nope. That one's too hard." We got together about three times a week to dine with him, visit and sing. He recalled so many wonderful old songs. Dad always remained his gentle, happy self. In that we were blessed. Always and forever, I will be grateful for this wonderful man—for his kindness, strength and wisdom...for the love of my father.

Related writings: "THE MUSIC LIBRARY," "DAD AND HIS THREES," "SUZE ORMAN," "A GLIMPSE OF HEAVEN" and "ALASKAN GOLD."

Dad and Mom (Paul and Rena)

Mom snapped Dad and me at dinner. I was about 26, and visiting
their home after work, wearing my bank uniform.

Dad in front of my Christmas gift. He was captain of "The Boulevard Stars,"
a street baseball team. I enlarged a tiny photo from those days.

Dad and me at the beach

Mom tried to "pose" us in their backyard. Dad was making funny faces,
I was laughing, and she decided to capture the comic moment.

SLOW MOTION

Did you ever feel that something in your life was happening in slow motion—when time and gravity appeared to be altered for a few brief moments? It did happen in the following instances. It happened for real.

One sunny day in 1963, during my sophomore year at the University of Southern California, I had just left French class and was pondering a personal instruction from our professor. He said I must learn to *think* in French, instead of forming a thought in English and translating the words into the French equivalent. For me, this seemed impossible. I was considering his suggestion, fairly oblivious to my surroundings, when the following occurred:

Deep in thought, with an armful of books (we didn't have backpacks in those days), I was walking across a very wide boulevard which had been closed to automobile traffic. Since I was used to people crossing it on foot, I didn't notice out the corner of my right eye a bicycle approaching at considerable speed. The young man pedaling plowed into me full force.

We wound up quite a mangled mess of wheels, books and note paper, with both of us sprawled face down on the ground. I still remember all these years later him shouting, "Oh my gosh! Are you all RIGHT?" He was genuinely concerned, and kept apologizing over and over. I told him I thought I was fine. We gathered up everything. The bike was still in working order. After we said our goodbyes, I continued homeward toward the dormitory, amazed that there were not any scrapes or bruises visible. I was emotionally shaken, but that was the extent of it. As I thought back over the experience during the rest of my walk, I remembered that during the incident, yes, I was aware of what was happening, but it was all so *soft and slow.* I saw the books fly out of my arms, but they seemed to be floating in air. When I fell, it was ever so gently, as if someone were cushioning the impact of the bicycle as well as my fall to the ground. Everything was in slow motion.

The second experience happened when my daughter Wendy was about two years old. We were in the backyard playing. At one side of our yard was a waterfall built by her father and me. It had two descending levels constructed of flagstone, each having sharp edges. Water would cascade over the flat stone surface and into the small pool below. There was a circulating pump at the bottom that pushed the water up through a hidden plastic tube to the top of the waterfall. The lower pool was about twenty inches deep with small rocks lining the bottom. We had cautioned Wendy not to go near the edge of the concrete decking adjacent to the lower pool.

This particular afternoon, we were playing with her ball when, *plop,* it bounced into the lowest pool of the fall. I was only about ten feet from our little girl. She chased the ball and did stop at the edge of the waterfall, but her forward momentum carried her into the lower pool.

I ran to catch her, but arrived too late. Scooping her up, I checked her over thoroughly to see if she was all right. Not one scratch or bruise was visible. She was just fine. While Wendy was falling, she seemed to tumble very VERY slowly, as if some unseen presence were *cradling* her into the water: Everything I saw was in slow motion.

The final occurrence (so far!) was when Wendy was in her late twenties, visiting from Kentucky. She had just left my second story apartment, and was already out in the parking lot, when I spotted a small box still sitting on the kitchen counter—my gift for Wendy. I felt I must catch her before she drove away.

Wearing a brand new pair of sneakers, I hurried out the front door, package in hand. At the top of the landing, even before I started to descend the concrete slab steps, the rubber on the toe of my shoe caught on the carpet outside the front door, and down I fell. My right hand reached out for the railing, but the weight of my body pulled it loose. Head over heels I went, down all fifteen stairs, finally landing with my nose only a few inches above the ground. Two moving men were passing by, carrying a dining room table to another resident. When I asked them to please help me stand up, they obliged and were very kind. This time there were a couple of scrapes and a few bruises, but nothing serious.

As I immediately recreated mentally what had just happened, I was amazed. In real time, that tumbling must have occurred very rapidly. Yet *this* is what I recall: In the beginning, I thought to myself, "Oh no, please help me! (calling out to God)…I mustn't let my head hit the stairs. If it does, I could wind up in the hospital!" The descent happened so *slowly*. As soon as my eyes fell upon a step looming in front of me, I was able to put out my hand and push off that step so my head wouldn't hit it. Then, as the next step approached, again I put out my hand to prevent my head from striking it. Down and down, these actions repeated themselves, all the way to the bottom of the fifteen steps. I was sprawled head first downward on my stomach, with my face just barely above the ground, before finally coming to a stop.

While reliving this experience in the moments that followed, I realized it seemed to have happened so slowly that time and gravity had somehow been suspended during the fall. Had anyone been a witness, surely it would have looked as if everything was happening in *real time*, this tumbling over and over all the way down the steps. No one was there *in the moment* but me, the delivery men having arrived just after the fall. Surprisingly, there were no broken bones, no huge gashes from the rock-hard cement, no concussion from my head hitting the steps—amazing. I felt very lucky, very blessed.

Thank you for indulging me in the telling of these stories. Maybe in your own life you will remember similar occurrences: moments when God, the Force, Angels, or whatever unseen presences, come with grace and compassion to cushion us from serious injury—perhaps because we still have more productive things to accomplish, and it just *isn't our time* to be hurt.

A GLIMPSE OF HEAVEN

For so many people, the subject of death is something they would just as soon not talk about. But in the case of my father, Paul Wright, there were some really beautiful and rewarding experiences during and after the time of his passing. This is a positive, uplifting piece, relating those occasions from his daughter's point of view. Other family members will have their own recollections. As for me, I remember the *positives*.

Dad spent his last years at a beautiful hilltop care center especially built for the needs of Alzheimer's patients. Mom and I visited him two or three times a week. Ultimately, he contracted pneumonia. We were told, after he was hospitalized, that the next few weeks would be his last. One interesting miracle—originally, Dad was brought to a hospital that was not listed on my parents' medical plan. His nurse during that brief stay turned out to be my long-time neighbor, Judy. Our apartments share a common wall.

Having learned much from the experience of Carol, my loved one who had passed earlier, we immediately transferred Dad to the San Diego Hospice. We were familiar with the respect given to each patient, as well as a staff devoted to providing comfort and freedom from pain. My two brothers, Bob and Will, flew in from Nebraska and Florida. Along with Mom and my daughter Wendy, we all kept vigil.

Returning to my apartment the first night was difficult. I kept wondering, during a fairly sleepless time, how Dad was doing. I had lived at the hospice with Carol in her expansive room, sleeping on the sofa which made into a queen-size bed. The second day of his stay, I packed a bag and moved in with Dad. Instead of wondering how he was doing, I could just glance over from my bed to see if he was all right. It worked out well. He still remembered who I was.

One night, about 2:00 a.m., two nurses came in to turn Dad. Waking up with these strangers was confusing to him. I was able to climb out of bed, stroke his forehead, and share that I was in the bed a few feet away, and that it was time for both of us to go back to sleep. "Okay?" He nodded and softly closed his eyes.

Dad could no longer speak, but he could mouth words silently, nod and shake his head. A cherished moment occurred one morning while holding his hand. He looked into my eyes, smiled and mouthed the words, "I love you so."

Dad lived at the hospice for about a week. During this time, my brothers Bob and Will looked after Mom. The three of them would arrive in the morning, stay until early evening, and then return to her apartment. It meant so much to have them taking care of Mom. She was emotionally fragile during this "long goodbye." Mom and Dad had shared 63 years of marriage. She spent many meaningful moments holding Dad's hand and talking to him.

On one occasion, while we were alone, Dad mouthed the word "Mom." He sometimes called our mother Rena that. I asked him if he wanted Rena. He shook his head. "Do you see *your* mom?" He nodded.

One special evening, as we were getting ready to go to sleep, I sat by Dad's bed. His eyes were closed. I asked him softly, "Do you know what I always loved most about you, Dad?" It wasn't the money he earned, the nice homes and material blessings he provided for his family (though I thanked him for all his hard work in that regard). "It was your heart, your kindness to everyone and the animals and birds. I loved most of all the things you taught me from your heart." His eyes sprung open. He looked at me and smiled with happy surprise. Then he closed his eyes. It felt as if he was saying, "You see the real me."

Another night, my friend Dennis, a very spiritually gifted man, came to offer some moral support. He and I were sitting in chairs, our backs against the window, keeping watch over Dad several feet away. On the other side of his bed was a CD player emitting soft instrumental music. Suddenly, Dennis exclaimed, "*Wow! Did you hear that?*"

I asked him, "What?"

He said the CD music had suddenly become very loud, then softened again. I told him I hadn't noticed any change in volume. He asked, "What song is playing?"

"*Unforgettable*…you know, an instrumental version of the one Natalie Cole recently recorded with an old soundtrack of her dad, Nat King Cole. It's a duet."

Dennis wondered why he had suddenly become aware of the increase in volume. Maybe Dad was unforgettable? After we tried to determine the significance of the song, Dennis finally suggested, "Well, just remember what happened. Maybe an answer will come later."

Meals were provided for family members. One morning, having finished breakfast in the lounge outside Dad's room, I returned to his bedside. As I rounded the corner of the room and his bed came into view, there was Dad with a big grin on his face, staring halfway up the wall just beyond the foot of his bed all the way to the ceiling. I pulled a chair up next to his bed and watched as he looked up and down, up and down, up and down. He was beaming. "Do you *see* something, Dad?" He nodded, still smiling. "Something tall?" Another nod. "Buildings?" A shake of his head. "Mountains?" (yes). "Do you see any people?" (yes). "Do you know who they are?" (no). "Do they look like people you would like to be with?" (yes). "Do you see bright white and yellow light all around?" (yes). It seemed he might be glimpsing heaven. Many have read or heard of such visions by patients when earthly death is approaching. People are "getting ready" to go back to their eternal Home. Wishing him to remain in the happy bliss evident all over his face, I asked one last question before being silent: "Does it look like HOME?" He nodded. He had a look of rapture on his face for a good twenty minutes. It's been years since that encounter, but the conversation is as fresh now as in 2000. I'll never forget it.

Eventually, the day arrived when Dad crossed over. My brothers took care of Mom while my daughter Wendy and I looked after his body through the process of transfer from the hospice. I gathered up my clothes and drove back to my apartment to get some sleep. It had been an emotionally draining day for all of us.

Having slept for only a few hours, I awoke with a sudden burst of energy. Further sleep seemed impossible. It was about 8:00 p.m. I decided to run a few errands. After all, the bank ATM was still open, and the cupboards were bare. I hurried to my van and turned on the radio. The tune playing was *Unforgettable* by Natalie Cole.

I called Dennis the next morning. He shared that to him it made perfect sense. This song was a love letter from a daughter to her dad who had passed away. It seems sometimes Forces in the Universe, whatever we wish to call them, arrange events into a wonderful dance of synchronicity, assuring us we are not alone. This book is filled with such remembrances, so many *miracles*. Perhaps the reader has volumes of his or her own to relate. I'm very glad I wrote the above occurrences down each day at the hospice. They were so special.

There is a second series of wonderful happenings related to Dad's passing. Our family had never experienced a "scattering at sea." Some years before, Mom and Dad had settled upon this method of "putting to rest" their final remains. None of us knew what to expect. Would it be a big boat with lots of families, each with a container of ashes? We were told to report to a certain coastal dock location in San Diego. My daughter Wendy and her husband would drive Mom. I would meet them there. A supermarket about a mile from my apartment had a floral section. I stopped that morning to purchase a whole bunch of flowers, enough to fill four brown paper grocery bags…flowers to cast upon the ocean waters.

Having reached the shoreline location, I spotted our little family. By that time, my brothers had returned home back east. As I lugged the four bags filled with flowers, Mom said, "Oh, honey, that's way too many flowers!"

Eventually, we all climbed aboard a small boat which carried our family, the captain and his assistant. This would be a very private affair indeed! The captain explained that we would motor out for about ten minutes. Then he would cut the engine and give us as much time as we needed.

It was a spectacularly beautiful day. As we journeyed out from the dock, the sky was blue with puffy, white clouds. The boat sat low in the water, and we could feel the cool mist of the ocean breeze on our faces. Seagulls were flying high above, emitting their raucous calls. We passed flagged floating buoys with seals relaxing on them. The natural beauty all around was so uplifting

When far from land, the captain cut the engine. He said he and his mate would climb to the front of the boat and sit there until we were finished. He advised that, because of the wind direction, we needed to put everything into the water on the right side of the boat. We had brought some special pieces to read: Psalm 23, Psalm 27, John 3, The Lord's Prayer, and the Statement of Being (a Christian Science reading which Dad could still recite, even in the depths of Alzheimer's: "There is no life, truth, intelligence nor substance in matter. All is infinite Mind and its infinite manifestation, for God is All-in-All. Spirit is immortal truth; matter is mortal error. Spirit is the real and eternal; matter is the unreal and temporal. Spirit is God, and man is His image and likeness. Therefore, man is not material. He is spiritual.").

I asked Mom, seated at the back of the boat, what she wished us to do next.

"Well, I want you to do the ashes. But first, put some flowers in the water, then the ashes, then the rest of the flowers."

When we had completed all her wishes, I handed Mom a surprise; one long-stemmed red rose for her to cast upon the water. She seemed pleased with that. Mom and Dad had been married 63 years.

There followed a few moments when we were each lost in our own thoughts. Suddenly Mom shouted, "Oh, LOOK!"

She was pointing off to the left side of the boat. To our amazement, there, floating out to the horizon, were an abundance of beautiful sun-kissed, multi-colored flowers, dancing on the waves.

"Oh," smiled Mom, "You didn't bring too many flowers after all...."

We notified the captain. He and his mate prepared to take us back to shore. Our return trip was equally as uplifting. Everything seemed so *alive* with the birds, the seals, and the sea mist. I decided that very day to follow Dad's example, and pre-paid all my own ultimate expenses up front, including the boat!

After our adventure at sea, we had lunch at *The Fish Market*, an oceanfront restaurant perched on the harbor in San Diego. Mom smiled the whole time. On a day which many might expect to be filled with sadness, we instead found so much beauty, love and joy. I recommend it highly.

Related writings: "THE LOVE OF MY FATHER," "DAD AND HIS THREES," "THE MUSIC LIBRARY" and "SUZE ORMAN."

"AND A LITTLE CHILD SHALL LEAD THEM"

Having enjoyed the experience of being a baby "cuddler" for ten years at a local San Diego hospital neonatal intensive care unit, I had only written one descriptive piece about the babies… until now. Something occurred that seems worthy of memorializing so that others may read about it and share in this wonderful adventure.

Shortly after I entered the NICU one evening, a nurse summoned me to a gliding rocker and placed a lovely baby girl in my arms. "She's only eight hours old," the nurse said softly, "and wait until I tell you her story."

It seems this little one was delivered to a drug-addicted mother who informed the delivery room staff she did not wish to see or hold her new baby girl. The mother asked them to just take her baby away. The little one arrived on this earth without anyone to love her. She received nourishment from a bottle instead of natural mother's milk from a source of warmth, love and caring. There were also some issues with the birth family which might complicate this child's chances of ever being adopted.

Looking into her sweet little face, I thought, "So you have been born with two strikes against you, nobody to love you, and perhaps years of foster care in your future." This little girl was, I think, of Scottish extraction, judging by her last name. She didn't look like a newborn. The baby had a peaches and cream complexion without the redness and wrinkles usually apparent after birth. The nurse shared it might be up to the people in the nursery to provide her with a first name. I offered "Molly," which seemed to suit her. Combined with the surname, it made her whole name sound sort of musical.

Gazing into her face for those few hours, I thought of all the thousands of hopeful parents who would be thrilled to adopt a baby as lovely as "Molly." Silent prayers were offered from that rocking chair. They included hopes that she would find a gentle life, surrounded by peace, joy, caring, and people to love, who would surely love her in return.

Soon little "Molly" was peacefully sleeping. Her closed eyelids revealed the baby was in REM ("rapid eye movement") sleep. Her eyes, while closed, were darting to and fro and she had the biggest grin on her face. I called the nurse over to ask what might be going on. This particular nurse had been in a terrible accident some nine years before. Her back was broken in several places. She broke her legs and other bones, and suffered internal injuries as well. She was told she would probably never walk again. Yet here was this dedicated nurse, working twelve-hour shifts. She was a very spiritual person, much of her belief having been strengthened by her own miraculous recovery.

The nurse looked into the baby's face and offered, "Well, she hasn't been on earth long enough to be all that happy about what she has encountered here thus far. I'll bet she's being entertained by angels or remembering the heavenly home she just left and how happy she was there." Her cheerful little grin, along with rapid eye movements, lasted for quite a while.

I've held little ones who were coming off of addictive drugs their mothers had taken. There were symptoms exhibited by them that I did not see in "Molly." Some people think drug babies are only "happy" because of the drugs. My own faith tends to believe the angel theory. Maybe this little one, who could not communicate in words, was validating for all of us that we come from a joyful and loving place before being born into this world.

"Molly's" story has a very happy ending. An attorney got involved. The baby was born on Thursday morning: by late Friday, a loving family had arrived from the East Coast to take their new little baby girl home. Nurses later shared that the family was very nice, and also had other children.

May God bless and keep little "Molly." May this little newborn grow and thrive. Perhaps one day, as an adult, she may wish to find her biological mother, and be a wonderfully positive influence on the woman who had given her up so many years before.

A happy postscript: Soon after writing this, I spoke with the nurse who was in charge of little "Molly" the day the family came to pick her up. The birth mother decided to hold her baby for a while. She also told the adoptive family how much she appreciated their providing a future for her daughter. They exchanged hugs and the family left for the East Coast. May God bless them every one….

Related writing: "HONORING THE TINIEST AMONG US."

DAD AND HIS THREES

My wonderful father, Paul M. Wright, was born March 30, 1910. He passed away (with all of his family gathered around) on February 3, 2000. My older brother Will's birthday is February 2nd. Our mother, Rena, mentioned to me that she had been praying, "Oh, please don't let him pass on Will's birthday." He didn't. Dad made his transition on February 3rd at 2:33 p.m.

Soon after he had passed away, I began noticing 33s on my clocks. Whenever I would check to see what time it was, it would be 3:33 or 1:33, 2:33, 8:33, 10:33, or whatever. I hadn't ever noticed that previously in my life. It made me wonder if there were other threes in Dad's past or in the present. Perhaps this was a "sign" he was watching over us.

I began compiling a list of facts from his life:

He was born 3-30-10.

He passed away 2-3-2000 at 2:33 p.m.

He and Mom had 3 children.

They were married 63 years.

During a critical time in my life involving a legal case, I knew the evidence was on our side, but the proceedings dragged on for a few years. Dad, over time, lent me a total of $30,000. When the case was over, I wrote him a check for $33,000 because I thought he deserved a 10% return on his investment. Pride insisted I pay him, not Dad! The amount is interesting, even though the $3,000 was not accepted. He and Mom didn't wish to take the added "bonus."

Another chapter in this book is all about Suze Orman, the famous financial expert, and it describes the influence her personal advice had on our family's structure of a revocable living trust that was established from the inheritance of my parents' trust proceeds (the result of Dad's lifetime of hard work). Suze Orman's name has 9 letters in it (3 threes). The name of the financial advisor she recommended has 12 letters (4 threes). His suite number is 3300. And the trust attorney she recommended is named Janet (my name at birth).

Hmmmmm. I wonder—Is the Universe smiling?

Finally, Dad was a Christian Scientist. He would always counsel that if a person gave the body proper nutrition and rest, the body had the capacity to heal itself. He did believe in the setting of broken bones and dentistry, but did not use novocaine…(ouch!). Two years ago, I began going to an acupuncturist who explained, "Acupuncture doesn't heal the body. Rather, the needles open up the natural energy pathways of the body, allowing the body to heal itself."

I believe Dad would have approved this natural healing method. The acupuncturist's phone number ends in 333. I found her through a "chance" conversation with a total stranger in a restaurant. A mere coincidence? Who knows? Maybe Dad was steering me in the right direction. I'll have to ask him one day when I cross over.

My own life path according to numerology is 30/3.

I was born 3-8-1945 at 3:30 pm

I still see Dad's threes all the time on so many occasions. It has been eleven years since his passing. For me, these constant reminders convey the measure of his devotion to his children. All three of us continue to benefit financially from his many years of hard work. He was a gentleman and a gentle man of kindness, honesty and good humor. He took care of his family and, to my way of thinking, is still doing so....

Love you, Dad.

Postscript:

The evening after first writing this piece, I fell fast asleep, facing the bedroom window. Later, I suddenly awoke and turned over, casting a drowsy eye at the digital clock across the room. It read 3:33. Perhaps a happy *hello*? It is these little mysteries of life that keep me optimistic—and always make me smile.

Related writings: "THE LOVE OF MY FATHER," "THE MUSIC LIBRARY," "SUZE ORMAN," "A GLIMPSE OF HEAVEN," and "ALASKAN GOLD."

Dad's favorite picture displayed on his business office desk.
Left to right: Me, Mom, Dad, brother Will, and brother Bob.

THE MOST WONDERFUL MIRACLE OF ALL

The most wonderful miracle of my life began in college with a color magazine photo. It depicted a little blonde girl about two years old, holding a daisy under her chin. This cutout adorned my dorm room wall. In private thoughts, I considered it impossible that a college freshman with dark brown hair could ever give birth to a child with tresses the color of sunshine.

Time passed, with a marriage at age 28. Then, wonder of wonders, the spectacular spring day, April 28, 1975…the day little Wendy Joy was born. While being driven to the hospital, I noticed yellow mustard flowers, the bright color of daffodils, blanketing the hillsides of San Diego. I made a mental note to always remember their beauty. Now, each spring, yellow decorates the hills all around as a happy reminder that a very special birthday is coming.

It was a natural childbirth with no drugs. She weighed nine and a half pounds. I remember sharing with her father, Richard, "It feels like giving birth to a watermelon!" Natural childbirth seemed the way to go in those days. Advocates of this method cautioned that any drugs going into the mother would also enter the baby. Sometimes, these caused an unpredictable amount of deterioration of intelligence. I wished her to begin life with every advantage. I also wanted to experience what natural childbirth felt like. Previous women through time immemorial had done it. It seemed like a *rite of passage* to experience all those feelings, both physical and emotional. When she first emerged into the bright light of the delivery room, I softly whispered, "Hi, Wendy!"

Her dad Richard had light brown hair, and, as fate would have it, there were blondes in his family. My own father Paul, though brown-haired, had been a towhead when young. One can fairly well guess what came next. As Wendy grew, she resembled the sunny-haired toddler from my college days (but even more beautiful, in this mom's opinion).

So many stories are going through my mind as I write this. They could fill volumes. With apologies to Wendy, only a few will be told, because they represent the depth of her mother's gratitude for the blessing of such a wonderful child.

At an age when little ones can barely articulate "Daddy" and "Mama," Wendy and I were at home one afternoon when Richard called from his office. While on the phone (remember wall phones?), he suggested we all go out for dinner that night. He encouraged me to choose a restaurant, something I was "in the mood for." Though I didn't say a word out loud, in my mind I was thinking about Chinese food. As I hung up, Wendy toddled up to me and pulled on my pant leg. "Chinee foo!" she proudly exclaimed. I was awestruck, knowing she had not heard me say those words. Science speaks of the special bond that exists between parents and children. That afternoon's experience would suggest perhaps a psychic connection is a part of that bond.

During elementary school, Wendy was in a program for gifted children. She was always self-driven. No one ever had to urge her to finish homework. She loved learning and being the best she could be. There were times she would help classmates with their work. She had a lot of patience, and seemed to be a natural-born teacher.

At San Diego State University, Wendy was awarded a Bachelor's Degree Magna cum Laude in Classics (Latin, Greek and ancient history), along with a Phi Beta Kappa Key. A paid fellowship to the University of Southern California led to her Master's Degree. She taught Latin at USC and San Diego State, while also tutoring home-schooled children. She understands six different languages. As I write this, Wendy is now a single mom, mother of three-year-old Jack, finishing her credential program, with hopes of becoming a high school teacher of Latin and English. She explained to me that although she can still seek a Doctorate Degree, her heart is really in teaching rather than in the thin, rarified atmosphere of academia. She gets such a thrill when a student who is struggling finally "gets it." She loves distilling difficult concepts down to where they can be easily understood by all her students.

As magnificent as her mind is, most impressive to me is the softness of her heart. She has incredible empathy and kindness. I have observed this limitless heart at times of caring for others (both human and animal), and in her patience with me (at times a real "fuddy duddy," still trying to watch over her child, who is now a grown woman). Jack has a wonderful mom. She anticipates his every need. Their bond is extraordinary to witness.

Wendy is incredibly loyal and giving to all those she loves. She has a great connection with her dad, who I'm sure could tell countless stories himself. I don't know these, as we are no longer married. She has stood by my side in good times and trying ones. After her grandpa (my dad) passed away at the San Diego Hospice, I said goodbye to Mom and my brothers who would take her home. Wendy and I said goodbye as well, or so I thought. I would stay in the room to watch over Dad's body during preparation for transport from the hospice. Wendy said goodbye to her grandma and uncles and came right back into the room. She elected to stand there by my side. She was 24 years old, very brave for a young person. So many people are afraid of death. I will always remember her courage, which so touched my heart, and her company that meant the world in those moments. When my loved one, Carol, passed away nearly two years earlier, I was in the wide hallway of the same hospice, phoning people to let them know she had made her transition. I called to ask Wendy if she would come help me take my clothes home, as I had been living there 24/7 for three weeks. I had not let tears flow, trying to do what was necessary to preserve Carol's dignity. This moment in time was all about her. My tears could wait. After hanging up the phone, having informed another friend, I saw Wendy approaching down the wide, carpeted hallway. As we hugged, out came all the pent-up tears. While she held me, I remember sharing, "I haven't fallen apart yet. I don't know why I'm crying so hard *now*." She replied, "Because you *can* (it's safe with me)." Carol's body was still on the bed. Wendy leaned over and kissed her forehead—again, such courage in the face of death. She had just turned 23.

Wendy wonders why I give her so many tips about nutrition, and say prayers all the time for her and little Jack, with added ones when they are traveling. It's because she's so precious to me. It's such a privilege to share love with one so unique and genuine. I can't imagine a world without her or Jack. Because of the eternal nature of life, I realize our connection will always remain. As spiritual beings, it takes only one thought of the other and we are *there*. What a comfort. Thank you, Creator of All.

Love and thanks to you, Wendy, for being the most special of all the miracles mentioned in this book…the most *wonderful* miracle of my life.

Related writings: "WATCHING THE NIGHT FALL," "SLOW MOTION," and "ON HOLDING MY DAUGHTER FOR THE VERY FIRST TIME" (a poem).
"DAD AND HIS THREES" tells another true story into which the following facts might fit nicely: Wendy and I were both age 30 when we gave birth. The day I wrote this story, she was 33, I was 63, and Jack was 3 years old.

Postscript: February 20, 2011: Wendy is now a member of the faculty at a San Diego District high school. At the age of thirty-five, she is thrilled to have a full-time teaching position, providing steady income for her and little Jack, who just turned five years old on December 6, 2010. She teaches Beginning Latin and Advanced Placement Latin, as well as three tenth grade English classes. It's a blessing to find a profession one loves and get paid for it, especially in this fragile economy. You GO, Wendy! Know my love goes with you…*always!*

Mouseketeer, age 2 ½

Little *ham*, age 3

Just relaxing, age 5

This photo appeared on the front page of a local newspaper. The photographer was visiting the YMCA summer day camp next to our apartments, and decided Wendy typified the campers. He gave us the "original" photograph. It's one of my "faves."

On one of my birthdays. Wendy was a teenager, being silly.

Wendy and her son, Jack (a teachable moment)

Wendy's resume picture

Wendy relaxing at my place.

1963...THE MOUSE...AND ME

In late summer of 1962, I arrived at the University of Southern California from Nebraska, not knowing a soul. Freshman year was exciting. By the spring of 1963, it was time to seek employment for summer break. Some friends in the dorm were applying to Disneyland. It sounded like a fun idea, one I never would have thought of on my own. I completed an application, and was thrilled when told to report to the Carnation Ice Cream Parlor on Main Street for an interview.

Punctual as always, with hopes as high as any 18-year-old's, I arrived as scheduled for the interview. "We are so sorry," was the response, "We accepted more applications than we have positions. We cannot even interview more people right now." Most applicants would likely have been disheartened, but then the optimism of youth took over. Should I give up and go home? No. I remember walking out of the ice cream parlor, turning to my left, and strolling down the street in search of *where* I was to work in Disneyland. It never occurred to me that I would not find a job. There it was, the happy, outrageous dream of youth, which could not be denied.

Just a few steps further took me to the *Enchanted Tiki Room,* which would be opening shortly as a new attraction. I told the manager about the Carnation experience, and asked if he would hire me for the summer. He looked me up and down and said, "Okay. Fill out one of our applications. You can have the job, but you must make me a promise. I want you to lie out in the sun each day and get a nice tan. Then you can work the evening shift from 5:00 p.m. to 1:00 a.m. Do you have a Social Security card?"

"No, sir."

"Well, get one of those and report to the employees' entrance on your first day. We'll let you know when that is. You'll be given a badge with your photo in costume on it. Each day bring sandals when you report for work. You'll be sent to wardrobe to pick up a sarong, a lei, and a flower to wear behind your ear."

That was that. To him, the process was matter-of-fact, routine. To me, it marked the beginning of a beautiful summer, filled with exciting, happy experiences. God bless him. A *yes* right there, on the spot, at the very first business I applied to after Carnation.

Most things were politically incorrect by today's employment standards. I was asked to tan up because others hired were Asian or Hispanic, in keeping with the tropical motif. No background checks or references were required. He said "yes" before I filled out the application. Later, after being hired, I was asked to go onto the back lot to meet with the union representative. Seated at a picnic table, he handed me a document to sign for union membership. With the bravado of youth, I asked, "What if I don't *want* to join the union?" He made a little horizontal gesture with his index finger across his throat; implying in silence, no membership, no job. The little pen he offered flew across the signature line. I didn't even read what was written above.

It was a heady time. Not having a car, I found an apartment about a mile away. My roommate was a young woman from Stanford. She worked at the *Mickey Mouse Club,* and her fiancé worked at the *Mule Ride* in Frontierland. While I was conveniently at work in the evenings, they could enjoy some alone time.

The walk to and from work included crossing Disneyland's parking lot. It was HUGE, and very dark at night, with sporadic floodlights dimly illuminating the black asphalt all around. One early morning, after 1:00 a.m., I was walking home in this sea of dark pavement (nearly every car was gone by then), when a tiny mouse ran up and stopped abruptly right in front of me. The little one looked up as if to say, "What are *you* doing in my parking lot?" We stared at each other for a brief moment. Then he (or she) slowly turned and walked away; just ambling, not in any rush. Hmmmm. I wondered if his name was Mickey.

Fun things happened that summer. Walt Disney was still alive, and would tour the park in a little topless antique car. He was present the day the *Enchanted Tiki Room* opened to a group of press reporters from around the world. The show's opening called for one of the saronged ladies to tap the perch of Jose, an audio-animatronic bird, and say, "Wake up, Jose, it's SHOWTIME!" Jose would then suddenly come to life, and thus would begin the bird and flower extravaganza. Birds on their perches would move, their chests rising and falling with their breathing, their voices actually emanating from inside their beaks. It was the first time such a phenomenon existed in a theme park. In the movie *Mary Poppins,* at one point Mary (Julie Andrews) is holding a bird on her index finger. It moves and sings in the same fashion. Well, this day, Jose's perch was tapped, but he remained quiet and didn't wake up. Embarrassed in front of the world's press, Walt Disney came out of the *Tiki Room,* stood atop the front steps and yelled, "What is going *on?*" Eventually, engineers in operations beneath the enchanted showplace got things repaired, and all was well. The show *did* go on, and has been doing so ever since.

Mr. Disney was always gracious when stopping by. He'd engage in innocuous conversation such as, "When does the next show start?" He had a wonderful heart, and, as revealed in biographies about him, envisioned a park where fathers and mothers could take their children without paying a fortune. He kept a personal apartment above the fire station on Main Street where he could gaze out upon all the happiness he was giving to people.

A revealing story about Mr. Disney was circulating that summer. While visiting *Tom Sawyer Island* unannounced, he approached a young man resting his back against a wooden post, a straw hat pulled down over his eyes.

"Do you enjoy working here?" asked Mr. Disney.

"Mm-hmm," nodded the sleepy worker.

"Then don't you think you'd better ACT like it?"

Imagine the young man's surprise upon raising his hat and realizing who had spoken. The story shared by employees was that this particular worker was not fired, but merely chastised.

Mr. Disney was always referred to with much affection. I never heard a negative remark about him from any employee that whole summer.

I remember Aunt Jemima. *Aunt Jemima's Pancake House* had this wonderfully rotund woman (the perfect image of the motherly illustration on the box of pancake mix) standing outside the door, greeting people as they entered. She was a true delight, with twinkling eyes and a sweet voice imparting lovely greetings to every visitor. Again, in today's society, her presence would probably be deemed politically incorrect.

Our duties included serving Tonga Juice at a bar adjacent to the park walkway in front of the *Enchanted Tiki Room*. Once, when I had my back to the walkway, "Donald Duck" began talking to me. As I turned around, an older gentleman giggled, admitting he was the voice of Donald for Disney cartoons. Clarence Nash was yet another gifted person with a "twinkle," and seemed a very sweet man.

One night we received a phone call. Lucille Ball was on her way with about half a dozen children. She would be coming incognito, and did not wish any attention drawn to them. Employees were instructed not to act excited when she arrived. Soon, here she came in a hot pink sweater with matching capri pants. A pink scarf covering her very red hair was tied under her chin. She sat in the front row of the show. No one in the crowd knew she was there *until* Jose woke up (because it was SHOWTIME). She let out the biggest "Lucy" laugh. Suddenly the crowd, who all loved Lucy, began looking around for the source. I recall in that show, people were watching *her* more than the birds and flowers. She raved afterward, saying how much she enjoyed it. No one was helping shepherd the children she'd brought along...a neat lady.

A famous gentleman walked up to the *Tiki Room* one day. I stammered, "Oh my gosh, you're, you're...."

"Martin Balsam. My name is Martin Balsam. Please remember my name after this."

Ah, the anonymity of being a character actor. Many of you would recognize him in an instant if you saw his face on film. But how many of us can remember the names of these character actors who contribute so much? This is for you, Martin Balsam. Whoever reads this will remember your name, and maybe even *Google* your picture.

Actor Jack Lemmon came while I was off one evening. Fellow workers said he showed up in a white tee shirt with a few days' scruffy growth of beard. Just like anyone else, he was relaxing on a summer night in Disneyland.

For an eighteen-year-old, it was such an exciting summer: Roaming the back lot, reporting to "wardrobe," seeing Pluto coming toward me, carrying a costume head under his arm, or Goofy, or the Three Little Pigs, and so many other characters. What fun seeing the little husband and wife (who portrayed Mickey and Minnie Mouse) exiting the employees' entrance in their long black limousine. The wee little elderly lady gymnast who played Tinkerbell "flew" each night, holding on with one hand to a long cable strung from the top of the *Fantasyland Castle*, waving her sparkling, magic wand to begin the fireworks.

There are lots of other stories, but this writing may be going on too long. I just wanted to relate how it was in a time of real freedom and trust in one another, when we could all indulge our innocence without the tight security present in today's society. This was the summer of 1963. In November, with the assassination of President Kennedy, everything would change. Our naïveté would sadly perish afterward, out of necessity in a changing world. The summer of 1963 was a truly magical time during which Mr. Disney used his creative imagination to realize a personal dream come true. And, for a little while, when traveling in his world, *our* dreams came true as well.

Postscript: No pictures exist "in costume" from that summer. The only one was on the identification badge, which was turned in before returning to college. What a silly, youthful mistake—no sense of history. Why didn't I think to take a *picture?*

HONORING CAROL

Words on a church wall in Upwaltham, England:
I will not wish thee riches, nor the glow
of greatness, but that wherever thou go
some weary heart shall gladden at thy smile,
or shadowed life know sunshine for a while.
And so thy path shall be a track of light,
like angels' footsteps passing through the night.

Dear Reader,

This is a different type of writing, and has a brief back story. It's the two-part eulogy given at my life partner Carol McKievick's memorial service on May 24, 1998.

Why offer it to you? First, Carol was (and is) an incredible soul. Secondly, she knew that in high school I had lost my voice right in the middle of giving a talk in speech class. Since that trauma, I had never again spoken in front of a group of people. In the hospice, as she was planning her memorial service, Carol confided she didn't wish anyone to give her eulogy but me. I gently reminded her of the earlier traumatic teenage experience. She smiled, "I know. Just write something on a piece of paper and read it into the microphone. Don't worry about gesturing or being a great orator. Just read it out loud."

It was impossible to deny the request of the love of my life while she was dying. Love overpowered any hesitancy. So I agreed to honor her request. I suspect a bevy of angels was present, giving me strength and ideas to compose her tribute. Uppermost in my own mind was to write something totally true, giving dignity to Carol, while also sharing stories that touched me most about her character.

You may wish to read it slowly and thoughtfully, as that is how I delivered it. After returning to my seat, 23-year-old daughter Wendy whispered, "Way to go, Mom. There's not a dry eye in the house." That filled me with confidence. Carol gave me a wonderful "gift" by insisting I face my fears. If I could deliver something that emotional, it might even be possible to speak before a group as large as the United Nations and not be nervous. You see, it's all about the people we honor, not about us, the speakers. What a *wonder* it is that I can now sing solo in front of people as well!

One final reason for including the eulogy: If you wish to know this writer, it is necessary to know the person who lived in my heart for nine years and still resides there, keeping me company, even now. It's both an honor and pleasure to share stories from her exceptional life.

Included is a favorite picture. It was taken by me at Yosemite. Carol was leaning on the car roof, gazing at the falls, and was unaware of being photographed. You can see the rapture and happiness on her face. She always considered Yosemite her "cathedral."

Two important parts of her history for those of you who never met her: Carol was first chair French horn in the DePaul University Symphony in Chicago. Our big connection was music. An independent consultant in the San Diego business community, she advised CEOs, Boards of Directors, and agencies regarding insurance issues.

We were closeted as a gay couple. There would be many people from the business community at the memorial service. The challenge was to convey the wonderful person I knew without saying we were a couple, as if we were "best friends." It has now been twelve years, times have changed, and society has become more open and accepting. I feel in my heart she's fine now with sharing the truth of our lives together. Carol gave her permission to share our true story after ten years had passed.

Thank you for indulging me. Here she is, as best I'm able to describe her, my life partner, Carol Ann McKievick:

EULOGY
for
CAROL ANN McKIEVICK
May 24, 1998

Thank you all for coming. We are here today in celebration of a life most beautifully lived, that of Carol McKievick. During her time here on earth, she was a woman of such grace. She put us in touch with our own hearts, always made time for each of us when *we* needed it, and could make us laugh so hard at the absurdities of life. Her giggle about such things was truly infectious.

It is my belief that Carol's greatest gift was her ability to see what was good and worthwhile in each of us, and by her words and actions, made us recognize and acknowledge what she loved most about us. She made us feel so good about who *we* were. She lifted us up. What a wonderful gift.

When Chris, her minister, asked Carol what she would say if she could speak at her own memorial service, she responded, "I'd tell everyone how much I loved them, and have something funny to lighten the mood."

One of the things Carol would surely wish to do in expressing her love would be to thank everyone so much for the gifts she received during the past five months: personal visits, phone calls, letters, flowers, pots of homemade chicken soup, boxes of popsicles, beautiful sculptures and books, healing visits from ministers, foot massages, back rubs and gifts of music and song *live* at her bedside.

Each person who came reflected the diversity of those she was able to connect with in her life: children, teenagers, people in their 20s, the middle-aged and the elderly, Democrats, Republicans, Independents and (I believe) one anarchist. There were two dogs, flower children, straight people, artists, gay men and lesbian women. There were Catholics, Jews, Protestants and agnostics, business people, maintenance workers, her biological family and her adopted family …and various shades of the human race from lily-white to black as night.

Of course, all of these terms are labels we in society put on one another. If we can stick labels on produce in a super market, why not label people? Carol didn't go by labels. She knew that underneath we all have the capacity to feel emotions deeply. That is the common denominator among all people, our *feelings*. We all can have our feelings hurt. We also can have our feelings *healed* by the giving and receiving of loving thoughts one to another. Carol knew about this *inner core of commonality* in each of us, and treated it with respect and honor.

Many years ago, I wrote a poem, and in it I took a little poetic license with the English language.

The poem is entitled:

FRIEND

Let me friend you
And mother you
But let me try
Not to smother you
Let me laugh you
And cry you
Let me overcome
The shy you
Let me listen you
And hear you
Let me rest awhile
The weary you
Let me walk you
And talk you
And break apart
The rock of you
Let me smile you
And thank you
For you're like me
Who loves what's true
And do I cherish you?
Are you blind?
The answer's YES
Dear friend of mine.

We are all here to honor Carol. She walked this earth with such a generous spirit, giving to each person she met dignity and respect. It was astonishing to witness during her final days how many people came to visit. Most amazing of all was how many shared that, "Carol is my best friend." She had so *many* best friends. She had the *best* of friends.

With her friends, there were two things she especially loved to do. She loved to eat and she loved to travel. While dining out with her a few years back, I was always struck by the way in which she would eat only half her dinner, then meticulously arrange the rest in a take-home box. She made it look so delicious, because, you know, presentation is everything. Later, she would present the lovely meal to her mother Ellene, who lived with Carol and was bedridden because of a stroke. No matter how delicious the food was, she would only eat half and save the rest for her mom.

Family was important to Carol; her mother Ellene and brothers Tom, John and Peter. Her father had already passed away by the time Carol and I met.

Carol was also the only person I ever met who could tell you the best foods she had experienced, the restaurant and the city. Best baked potato, best creamed spinach, best fried shrimp. That last one was sitting on a dock in Galveston, Texas, eating freshly caught deep fried shrimp out of a paper sack. She could make you drool with her lavish descriptions.

While traveling, Carol never packed lightly. Before our first vacation, she warned me ominously, "I don't travel light." I packed one suitcase and some loose clothing. Carol took everything but the kitchen sink, which fortunately was tightly secured to the plumbing in her house.

I used to make fun of this habit, but wouldn't you know, some emergency would arise to which she would respond, "A left-handed Swiss Army knife with nail clippers? You know, I just happen to have one of those!"

"Cinnamon-Flavored Swiss Miss Sugar-free Cocoa? Do you want it with or without the little marshmallows? Yep, I have it!"

Well, Carol didn't pack lightly on her final journey either. When we all get on that train, we don't get to take anything with us, just the love we have given and received while here on earth. Once again, it's easy to imagine her confiding to God as she bundled her load off to heaven on May 9th, "You know, I don't travel light." It's also easy to imagine God being very pleased with the *baggage* she brought along.

Most of us spend our lives searching for one special person: One who knows us inside and out, and says all of it, *all* of it is just great; not only great, but beloved and totally worthwhile. What we ourselves consider a fault, this special friend finds endearing. Some of us never do find such a person. If we do, we are so blessed, not only to have loved them, but to have been loved *by* them.

We get one such friend in a lifetime if we are lucky. I feel, having known Carol, that I have used up my apportionment of one. Given the choice, I would do it all again in a heartbeat—go through all of the challenges and joys (yes, there were lots of joys) of the last five months just to re-live the wonder of the years we spent together. I have met in the past and shall meet in the future many extraordinary people. But I shall not meet the likes of Carol McKievick again here on earth. She trusts God, and I do too, that we will be reunited one day…and what joy that day will bring. Thank you, Lord, for your precious child, Carol—for letting each of us share in the wonder of her light and love of life.

Carol remarked when JJ the young whale was released into the ocean after recovering at Sea World, "Godspeed, JJ!" and she softly began to cry. You see, JJ was no longer in the care and control of human beings. We could not *help* her. She was on her own, adrift at sea, in the care of God alone.

Godspeed, Carol. May God speed you all the way *Home….*

(Later in the service, after musical selections and other speakers):

It seemed appropriate to set aside a few moments in the service to take note of Carol's wonderful affinity for nature. You will notice one of the charities she selected before her passing is the Feral Cat Coalition. She held a special place in her heart for those cats born in the wild, who roam our neighborhoods, just trying each day to survive. She herself would trap the wild ones, have them spayed and neutered, then return them to her neighborhood…so that little ones would not be born into a similar struggle for existence. Lucky the stray who found its way to Carol's doorstep. It was never turned away without a meal.

I remember so well one morning at the hospice. Carol was asleep and I was looking out the window at the sky and trees, the birds and flowers. I began to pray silently, "Oh God, what will I do without Carol to talk with every day?" Perhaps there is someone in your life about whom you feel the same. He reminded me to look to these things of nature…the plants, trees, flowers and sky; the animals, the ocean. He put them here for us as a source of beauty and comfort—for these are reminiscent of the beauty and grandeur found in heaven, our real and eternal Home. I believe now that whenever I look at a passing cloud, a beautiful flower, a breaking ocean wave, or a bird on the wing, I will remember Carol and see the beauty of her real essence there.

We all have a favorite spot in nature. For Carol, it was Yosemite. Ansel Adams, the best-known photographer of that park, said wilderness had always been, "A mystique: a valid, intangible, non-materialistic experience. Wilderness is not only a condition of nature, but a state of mind and mood and heart." Carol always said Yosemite was, for her, a *spiritual* experience.

Finally, on many evenings, if Carol was along and the moon was full over San Diego, we loved to get my binoculars from the trunk of the car and look at the lunar mountains and craters. The moon's white brilliance always shone so beautifully against the dark evening sky.

Because Carol so loved the world of nature and the world of music, we offer the following entitled, *I'll Be Seeing You*. It speaks of losing someone, then later finding comfort in beautiful and familiar surroundings. The lyrics of this well-known song are quite wonderful. We will be playing the instrumental version….

(Concludes Service)

Carol was gazing at the falls in Yosemite, and didn't realize I was taking her picture. See the rapture on her face? She always referred to Yosemite as her "cathedral."

On a lengthy west coast vacation in 1994, we stopped at a small roadside exotic animal sanctuary. The manager asked, "Would you girls like to do something few people in the world get to experience? I'll take your picture." We loved holding these adorable twin tiger cubs. Very special!

Carol and a special friend at the San Diego Wild Animal Park.

Carol at the Grand Canyon on yet another wonderful vacation.

WATCHING THE NIGHT FALL

As a young couple with a child on the way, my husband Richard and I purchased a lovely home in San Carlos, a suburb of San Diego. Much of its charm was due to an exceptional view out large picture windows spanning the back of the living room. The panorama swept across four small mountain ranges (or *hill ranges* might be a better description)—as far as the eye could see, just beautiful hills and sky.

After moving in, we fell more and more in love with the view. We installed a swimming pool (Richard's dream), a waterfall, and plenty of decking for lounging and enjoying the wonderful expanse of nature just beyond our canyon fence.

One summer evening at sunset, having come through a lovely but tiring day with our 2½-year-old toddler Wendy, I seized a moment when she was inside with her dad to take a restful break. While enjoying some quiet time, sitting on the deck and looking across the pool toward the mountains, I heard the sliding screen door open. Out came Wendy, who wondered aloud, "Mommy, what are you doing?"

Not wishing to break the enjoyable soft hush between sunset and twilight, I put my finger to my lips and whispered, "I'm watching the night fall." She uttered not a word and walked over to her own little chair, then quietly brought it over and set it down next to mine. I pointed out to her all the little birds flying from right to left just in front of us about twenty feet up in the air. "See? The birds are flying home to their nests to go to sleep for the night." We sat quietly, watching and listening to the sights and sounds of nature as twilight gently led us from sunset to darkness.

When night had come, and the evening stars were finally out, we made our way back into the house. Her dad then left to run an errand. It was Wendy's bedtime, but she didn't want to go to sleep just yet. I suggested we both go into the family room. She was so very tired, but like a typical toddler, would not surrender to the weariness. Wendy was too tired for a story. I put some soothing, melodic music on the stereo, and we settled in side by side on the sofa. The adult in me knew what would soon happen to this unsuspecting little girl. Within minutes she would be sound asleep.

The music soon began to work its magic. Having sat for a little while, pretty soon I felt her head lean into my upper arm. I looked down and her eyes were closed. She was softly breathing, and had fallen fast asleep.

It was a moment I have never forgotten, that sweet night of sharing quiet time with my little daughter. Whenever we did something wonderful as she was growing up, whether on vacation or in our own home town, I would say to Wendy, "We're making a memory." We surely made a lovely one that night.

I scooped her up, gently took her to her bedroom, and tucked her in. Bath time, brushing teeth, and story time could wait until morning. Waking her from this wonderful peace would be to disrespect her gentle slumber.

As the sun began to set the following evening, I realized Wendy must have also thoroughly enjoyed the quiet respite of the previous night. She toddled up to me and asked, "Mommy, can we go out again and watch the night fall?"

WHAT'S THE BUZZ?

A popular pet store at the mall seemed particularly inviting one day. My daughter Wendy was getting ready to leave home, and I was about to become a single mom with the "empty nest" syndrome. While I was growing up, my own mother never allowed her children to have dogs or cats. Still, every Christmas morning, I'd peek into the living room to see if there was a little puppy in a basket under the tree. It never happened. So it was always fun, while visiting a pet shop or animal shelter, to stop and see the puppies and kittens.

This particular day, I was walking past a table atop which nestled a little pile of gray and white mottled kittens. In the center of the little mound appeared one tiny head, raised up with eyes staring at me. As I meandered toward the back of the store, this little kitten turned its head, following me. When I came back by the table on my way out, it continued to gaze at me.

Something inside prompted me to ask the woman in charge if I might hold the little kitten. As I lifted him up and put him next to my chest, he buried his face into me, sort of nuzzling. Before I knew it, I had ordered a cat carrier, food, litter box, and all manner of kitty care things I knew nothing about. I had not found a kitten to adopt. He had found me.

Off the two of us went to our second story two-bedroom apartment. I knew Wendy would be home soon, so I put the little guy in her bathroom with a folded card table blocking the door. There he was with his litter box, food and water, complete with newspapers on the floor. He was about six inches long, a gray, white and black tabby—a pathetic, tiny little figure in his new huge environs, softly mewing.

Soon Wendy came home. I excitedly told her about the new member of our family. She was familiar with raising cats, having had that experience with her dad. She exclaimed that I couldn't just leave him there. "You have to love him up!" With that, she went in, sat on the covered commode, and held the little fellow on her lap, his tiny back lying lengthwise in the valley between her jean covered legs. She rubbed his head and tummy, and soon he began to purr—a good introductory lesson for Mom in how to make a kitty feel at home.

After a while, it was time for him to make his first "number two." He hopped up into the litter box, did his business, and covered it up. Amazing! His mama had taught him well. Later, in his second attempt, he didn't bury it. I silently pointed with my index finger to about one inch above the offending little pile. Kitty understood immediately, hopped back into the box, and covered it up. He was young, but so very *smart!*

Mr. Rogers was always a TV favorite when Wendy was small. I named the kitty Daniel after the character "Daniel Striped Tiger" on his show. They seemed to resemble one another.

When Daniel was about a year old, my partner Carol and I rescued a tiny kitten. She had been named "Buddy" by the children of a family who lived next door to Carol. They had suddenly moved away, and left her behind. I fell in love with Buddy at first sight, and happily brought her home. She was black with white blazes on her chest, face and tummy, and little white fur "socks" on her feet. Buddy grew up to be about half the size of Daniel. But as time progressed, she learned to rule the roost. She would lick the inside of Daniel's ears and the top of his head (I guess implying that he was in some sort of subservient position in the family. Or maybe she was just being a mama to him. Who knows? I'm not a cat.). After Wendy left home, it made the nest feel cozy once more to have these two new little friends.

After thirteen years had passed, Buddy suddenly developed a tumor inside her tongue. She got sick, was diagnosed, and then was put to sleep, all within five days. The veterinarian told me this was common among cats. He had never seen one recover from it, even after extraordinary surgical procedures. I held little Buddy on her back in my arms, softly telling her we were going back home where she could "see the little birdies" come to the terrace once again. I just kept talking to her about the little birdies and wearing a smile on my face, then nodded to the vet and he gave her the injection. She was gazing trustfully into my eyes when she expired. It was only then tears began to fall. I didn't want her to be worried at the moment she crossed to the other side. I do believe for certain our pets go to heaven. Buddy "came back" a couple of times in ways that were undeniable, but that's a whole other story.

The following year, Daniel came down with a tumor on his rear leg. This time, surgery was elected. He seemed okay after the six-week recovery ordeal had ended. But he had to wear a plastic cone around his head for three of those weeks. He hated it. I tried to keep it wiped clean, because his wet food would cling to it as he ate. Daniel always dreaded going to the vet, even for annual checkups.

In 2006, Daniel suddenly began groaning softly as if in pain. He stopped eating. The next morning, he was lying on his stomach on my bed and I got face to face with him and softly asked, "You're not feeling very good, are you?" He looked into my eyes as if to say, "Mommy, please make it go away."

Something inside my heart decided against making him go through more vet examinations and heroic procedures. "Maybe this is Daniel's time to leave you. If so, make it as gentle as possible."

I was able to locate Kristi Freeman, a veterinarian who specialized in euthanasia for pets, visiting the family home to perform this service. Thankfully, she could come to our apartment at noon that very day. When I opened the door, it became immediately clear she was a godsend for Daniel. Kristi was soft-spoken and unhurried in demeanor. She sat on our sofa and we visited awhile, waiting for Daniel to come out of the little bathroom cupboard, where he had secluded himself when the doorbell rang.

After about ten minutes, I opened the cupboard and announced softly, "Daniel, there is someone here to see you." Kristi stood at the door of the bathroom. Upon seeing her, he came right out. He seemed to sense that she was there to help him. She examined Daniel, listened to his symptoms, and agreed that it was a good time to gently put him to sleep. She advised the alternative would be to go through more surgeries at the vet. I didn't want him to leave me, but also didn't wish him to go through all the fear, panic, and physical pain of treatment.

Kristi explained that the first shot would make Daniel feel gradually sleepy. She suggested just letting him roam around the house until he started to stagger like a little drunk. That took about ten minutes. I was sitting in my recliner. I asked Daniel to come next to mommy and sit in his little, pillowed wicker basket. Never a lap cat, he often rested there while we watched TV, or the "birdies" on the terrace. I would gently pet him, and he would respond by softly purring. We had shared many such contented moments over the years. On this final occasion, Daniel got comfy in his basket and drifted off into a quiet nap. It was obvious he was sleeping peacefully, and not experiencing any pain.

Kristi then asked if there was a special place in our home where I would like her to administer the final injection to stop his heart. My quilted bed seemed a perfect place. I could sit next to him and speak softly while he passed. When he was still in the basket, I noticed that his purring had changed to a buzzing sensation against my hand. It was still a purr-like cadence, but *electric* instead. I asked Kristi if she felt it, and she answered, no. She sensed only the softness of his fur and his breathing.

While Daniel was asleep on the bed, she asked me to let her know when to give him his last injection. Finally, I nodded, and she stopped his heart. He was totally at rest and didn't even twitch during all of this. Kristi then went out to her truck to get a fresh towel, in order to wrap his body for later cremation.

Daniel and I were alone. I kept petting him, and once again noticed the soft electrical buzzing in the same cadence as his former purr. Logically, I knew he had passed. But still the buzzing continued.

When Kristi returned, I asked her once more to lay her hand on Daniel. Did she feel the buzzing? "No," she said, "just his fur." I stroked him again—*still* the electric purring.

She wrapped Daniel slowly with respect. I asked her what she thought the buzzing might be. She said it could be a love connection. "Maybe," she offered, "he's saying thank you...."

Thank *you*, Daniel and Buddy, my dear little friends, who taught me the meaning of a very *special* kind of love.

Daniel and Buddy keeping an eye on the world.

Why do guys always need to control the remote?

Daniel naps while Buddy keeps watch.

SUZE ORMAN

This true story is all about parental love and the kindness of strangers. In December of 2005, my mother Rena Wright was passing away in a Florida hospital while I was at home in La Mesa, California (a suburb of San Diego). Why was I not with my mom? Well, some months prior, we had spent a week together at her Florida assisted living residence (I occupied one of the empty apartments). At week's end, I smiled and asked Mom if we had been able to discuss "just about everything under the sun" during our wonderful visit. She laughed and agreed, "Yes, most definitely!"

Mom was still fairly agile, so I was surprised when, as I was leaving to drive to the airport, she remarked, "This will be our last time together here on earth. The next time we see each other will be in heaven." I feel very fortunate to have had such a heart to heart in-person visit with my mother, especially after she made that last comment. Some people never have such an opportunity before a loved one passes.

For that to be our final visit was my mother's wish, and I promised to respect it. Perhaps she wanted me to remember her as she was then, rather than frail in a hospital at the end of her life.

Whatever her reasons, Mom's time to leave this earth eventually arrived. A hospital nurse held a phone to her ear, and I was able to speak with her. She was very weak. The best I could do was to express my love. Though I wanted to fly to be with her, I needed to respect our agreement and my earlier promise.

A couple of months earlier, I had signed up for a free presentation by Suze Orman at the San Diego Convention Center. Someone recently told me she had never heard of Ms. Orman, so here is a brief description: She is a woman who began working as a waitress/fry cook and became, through much study and hard work, a premier financial expert of our time, and a multi-millionaire. She has written many books, runs a financial website, and has appeared on various news and information programs (*Oprah, Larry King*, etc.). Every Saturday night on CNBC, she hosts *The Suze Orman Show*, during which she offers advice to callers with questions about their personal finances. Suze says she cares most about helping people, answers questions when they approach her on the street, and promises to continue this work even after she retires from public view.

When the time for her lecture came that Friday in San Diego, I was worrying about and praying for my mother three thousand miles away. With Mom no longer able to communicate, it was just a matter of waiting for her to pass. She was ninety-two years old. Doctors said her heart was beyond any surgical repair. I could either worry about her in my apartment, or go to the lecture and worry about her there. Clear thinking wasn't exactly part of the scenario that day. Before leaving home, I sat down and wrote a brief letter to Suze Orman. Basically, it related there would soon be an inheritance coming to my two brothers and me. They were both financially savvy and enjoyed playing the stock market, but I was not gifted with as much expertise. The letter intimated how much I loved my parents, and did not wish to diminish their gift, because my dad had worked so very hard to earn it during his lifetime. It would not honor him to squander a penny of it by making foolish decisions regarding investments. Beneath the signature at the bottom of the letter were my address and phone number.

Off I went to the presentation. Upon arriving, I handed the letter to a woman wearing a badge. "Would you please give this to Suze Orman?" She nodded. The lecture was informative, but I kept thinking about Mom. On the drive home, I considered it probable the letter had wound up in a trash can. It seemed unlikely a person as famous and successful as Suze Orman would bother with a brief little letter from someone she didn't even know.

Mom passed away two days later on Sunday. It was difficult to honor her wishes and not be there by her side. On Monday night, the phone rang. A voice on the other end said, "You're not going to believe this, Janet, but it's Suze Orman."

She said there was something about the letter that so touched her heart, she just had to call. Suze offered much comfort, and revealed she had e-mailed the gentleman who handled her own personal finances. She advised him to wait for my call. Suze provided his name and phone number, but emphasized that the decision whether or not to speak with him would be totally my own. She gave an assurance that she would make not a penny from the referral, and promised he would not be one to take advantage by charging inappropriate fees or large commissions.

Our mother and father had a revocable living family trust. I wished to have something similar for my daughter Wendy and grandson Jack. Suze concurred, but was one step ahead already. She said she had also contacted a woman in California who had been her business partner for many years, and specialized in family trusts. Again, she assured me that she made not a penny from this referral. The trust attorney would charge a reasonable fee for establishing a will and revocable living trust. In Suze's words, "She won't rip you off."

Suze Orman spent forty-five minutes with me on the phone. This woman who was worth millions, and whose working moments were very valuable, set aside time to help a total stranger. Had she not done so, I suspect the inheritance from my parents would have been vulnerable to some decisions of my own, which may not have been very wise. As I write this piece in July of 2008, the United States economy is said to be in its worst shape since the 1930s. Yet the investments recommended by the wonderful gentleman in New York seem to be holding up better than most. For that I am very grateful.

On that special evening, Suze Orman, with her personal generosity, made my life so much easier, so much better than it might have been without her counsel. She proved, having weathered so many financial ups and downs in her own life, that she does indeed live by the credo with which she ends every Saturday night show on CNBC: *"People first, then money, then things."*

Since my dad Paul Wright passed away in 2000, I have noticed an abundance of number threes popping up in my life. Dad took care of our family all his adult life. He seems to still be taking care of us, both monetarily and with his positive *influence*, which lives on. I re-read my copy of the letter given to Suze Orman. To me, it didn't seem all that remarkable. I like to think Dad, on the other side, was influencing her thoughts as she read it. Oh, and the suite number of the gentleman who has been managing my accounts? Suite 3300. Go figure. Whether this sounds logical or not, *"Thanks, Dad...."*

Related writings: "THE LOVE OF MY FATHER," "DAD AND HIS THREES," and "A GLIMPSE OF HEAVEN."

Mom in Florida with sweet little Scottie belonging to her son Will and his love Dorothea

ALASKAN GOLD

On December 12, 2005, my mother, Rena May Wright, passed away. She had been lingering in a Florida hospital, waiting purposely for her great-grandson to be born in Kentucky. My daughter Wendy gave birth to Jack on December 6th. Though the blessed event was far away, Mom took comfort in having lived long enough to hear the good news.

Mom and my dad, Paul, had lived through the Great Depression, and were very conscientious with their savings. Dad passed away in 2000. The two of them had made provisions in a trust for proceeds to be divided equally among their three children.

In material terms, my life in La Mesa, California (a suburb of San Diego) had been lived rather simply. After nearly thirty years in the business world, I became disabled with fibromyalgia in 1992. Disability income covered basic living expenses. Upon receiving one third of our parents' estate in early 2006, I set up a trust with Wendy and Jack as beneficiaries. But, before doing so, I spent a small portion of the money to follow a dream.

Many friends and extended family members had shared with me the fun they experienced cruising to various parts of the world. I decided to see what all the excitement was about. There would likely be just this one cruise in my lifetime. Dad had worked so hard to earn this money. I wished to respect his efforts. He probably would have thought it okay to exercise this one indulgence. His own father had once spoken of a desire to sail to Australia.

In researching various trips available through AAA, my focus was on the "natural wonders" to be experienced. Eventually, I decided to venture north to Alaska. The travel agent shared that often passengers were envious of cabins with verandas. Princess Cruise Line had just launched a new ship on which every cabin with an outside exposure had its own porch. Viewed from onshore, there were several levels of verandas extending from bow to stern.

Having lost my life partner Carol in 1998, Dad in 2000, and Mom in 2005—mixed with the joy of young Jack entering our lives—it was a rather *contemplative* time. I chose to take the trip alone in early May of 2006. I wished to just relax and spend time observing the wonders of nature, alone with happy thoughts of loved ones, and memories of the previous 61 years.

This vacation account won't be a description of cities visited, tourist attractions, ports and dates, etc. Rather, I invite you to come along on a journey of deep wonder and exhilarating emotions; a *sensory* experience of beautiful Alaska.

There were many of the usual accoutrements onboard the ship: theaters, casinos, gift shops, spas, karaoke sing-alongs, etc. I tried to focus only on the natural wonders peculiar to Alaska that were not available back home. There were, of course, interesting conversations with other passengers during mealtimes. Companionship was always available if desired.

The veranda outside was spacious, with two tables, a chaise lounge, and two upright chairs. There was a half roof. Even if it rained, one could still sit out on the porch. I kept my binoculars and camera on one of the tables, always at the ready.

This adventure was in late spring (April-May). We were told that later on in summer, there are huge swarms of mosquitoes (that even leave shadows on the ground!) and an abundance of flies. But on this trip, all was beautiful and insect-free, with crisp, cool air. Delightful!

There were lots of trips ashore at ports of call. One morning we experienced a beautiful train trip up into the mountains, complete with breakfast in a domed car. We enjoyed waterfalls, deep canyons, lots of pines and interesting wildlife.

On a bus journey into the mountains, we saw two- and three-foot pine trees poking out from a white carpet of snow. Our guide asked, "How old do you think those little trees are?" The little bitty trees were 200-300 years old. They survived by being tiny. Snow covered them in winter, protecting them from strong winds.

Alaska is huge. The first day we learned there are over a million lakes throughout the state. Many are small, to be sure—but over a million! The permafrost is interesting, consisting of frozen subsoil found throughout Alaska. It is difficult to build permanent structures because, in warm weather, the permafrost melts slightly, and the ground becomes mush. Country folks are constantly relocating their outhouses, many of which are complete with ornate decorations, paintings on the walls, carpeting, etc. What fun.

Glaciers in Alaska are constantly moving. There are helicopter trips offering the chance to stroll their surfaces. At a place called Glacier Bay, the water is deep blue. There are hundreds of big floating chunks of ice with seagulls and seals lounging on them. The deepest layers of the glaciers are blue, an interior color visible when glimpsing their exposed edges.

Worth mentioning on this sensory journey, is Alaska's delightful atmosphere. The state is so far from large industrial cities that the air is like a healing *elixir*, intrinsically fresh, clean and crisp. My lungs felt so happy there. Some days, because of the clarity before our eyes, we could almost *see forever*.

At the Mendenhall Glacier in Juneau, there was a huge body of deep blue water. We were standing on land looking across the water toward the glacier (again, with lots of blue ice visible). A piece of that glacier had broken off and drifted across to the shore where many of us were standing. It didn't take long for each one of us to pose at the water's edge, while holding that chunk of ice in one hand—with the glacier forming a lovely backdrop across the bay. Noticing I was alone, a gentleman tourist offered to take my picture. It remains one of my favorites from the trip.

On another occasion, the ship was cruising slowly, following the coastline, preparing to pull into a port of call. From our porches, we could see a fish cannery onshore. It was just before sunset, and the business was dumping all its waste from that day's processing into the water. Fifteen bald eagles were flying all about, very excitedly diving into the water, and gobbling up the extravagant abundance of food. I knew there were fifteen because the young man on the veranda just above and to the right of mine was shouting, "There are fifteen! I counted 'em!" *Wow*. How often in one's lifetime does a person get to see a sight like that?

We were cruising out to sea one day, far from the coastline. I was lost in thought, drinking in the beauty all around. Suddenly from above and behind me, a bald eagle came swooping down, wings outstretched, across the porch and out to sea. Had I stood up from my chair, I could have touched its underbelly. The bird was so huge, and the moment so spellbinding, that I was frozen and couldn't grab my camera in time. Gasping in wonder was all I could do. Even now, I can see the eagle in my mind's eye as it flew majestically away from the ship and out over the ocean. *Spectacular!*

Another day, we were even further from terra firma, cruising at a fast clip, trying to reach the next port. Hummingbirds have always been special to me; they visit my porch at home every day. I was watching the whitecaps dancing atop the ocean waves, when suddenly a hummingbird came to my veranda and hovered right in front of me. My jaw literally dropped. "What are you doing way out here?" I wondered silently. It would be a very long trip for that little one to find its way back to land so very far away.

Where did it *come* from? The bird hovered for awhile, then buzzed off as they do; suddenly here, then just as suddenly gone. Sort of a *miracle* (at least it seemed so to me). I can still picture those moments in my mind: The bald eagle and the hummingbird…quite a pair of wonderful memories.

We stayed on land one day at the Copper Canyon Resort. Even though it was springtime with no snow on the ground, the hotel offered tourists rides with sled dogs in training. One of the thrilling "adventures" was to meet the dogs and pet them, then climb into a sled on wheels with another tourist. The trainer stood behind us, gave the dogs the "mush" command, and off we went, speeding along forested country roads. The dogs seemed to love running, even without any snow. We laughed like little children. It was so much fun!

The most extraordinary and rare experience I have saved for last. Prior to booking the cruise trip, there was an opportunity to reserve a seat on a small, twin-engine plane to fly over Denali (Mt. McKinley), at 20,320 feet, the tallest mountain on the North American continent. The word "Denali" comes from the native Athabascans. It means "The Great One" or "The High One." William Dickey, a gold prospector, renamed it "Mount McKinley" after President

William McKinley. Native Alaskans have long since been upset by that gesture. They say President McKinley had nothing to do with the mountain. So I will honor their history, and refer to the mountain as Denali. By the way, the origin of the state's name, Alaska, comes from the Aleut word "Alaxsxaq," meaning "Object toward which the action of the sea is directed," or "mainland." The travel agent explained that dense fog usually enshrouded the top of the mountain. There were only about six clear days in any given year when the flight could be safely made. I was a white knuckle flier, but signed up anyway, realizing that few individuals experience this adventure in a lifetime.

The day we checked into the hotel at Denali National Park, there was a note in my reservation envelope. The hotel no longer had a contractual relationship with the flight company offering tours over Denali. There followed a suggestion we sign up for some other activity during the time of the cancelled flight. I chose a bus tour through Denali National Park. There we would see forests and various species of wildlife and birds. It sounded stunningly beautiful to this nature lover.

We were on that tour the next morning, when the bus driver stopped to let us all out to photograph Denali. While standing next to me, he remarked that it happened to be one of those rare clear days atop the mountain (one of only about six per year). I sighed and told him our flight for that very day had been cancelled. He asked quietly if I would still like to go up. I said, "Of course!" "Well," he confided….He knew a couple of guys who might be able to take me up about 2:00 that afternoon. He told me to wait outside the bus after he dropped us all off at the hotel. He then pointed to a small office across the wide street, suggesting I inquire within.

Just as he had indicated, when I told the owners the story and asked if they could fly that afternoon, they said "sure" and we made a date for 2:00. A few of us gathered at the office and were taken by van to an airstrip outside of town. There we boarded a very small plane; the pilot, four other people and me. We all brought cameras to record moments only a few people each year get to experience.

Since my dad passed in 2000, I had been noticing *threes* on my clocks. I would check to see what time it was, and it would be 2:33, 10:33, etc. There is another true story in this book entitled, "DAD AND HIS THREES," all about other threes in his lifetime.

We taxied down the runway. At the end, we made a U-turn to the right. As we did so, I noticed a row of little shacks not too far away. On a tan-colored one, it looked as if someone had taken a spray can of black paint and written:

What time is it?

It's 3:33

TIME TO FLY!

I blinked in disbelief. This couldn't be real. I blinked a few more times, staring at it over and over. It was really *there!* Well, that gave me courage. I took it as some kind of *sign* that I shouldn't be afraid, no matter what happened in the next hour or so.

Oh, my. You know that word "turbulence?" Our tiny little plane was lurching all over the place. The pilot was playing the rambunctious tune from ABBA entitled, *Fernando*. We were soaring over a majestic mountain, gazing down at many snow-covered surfaces no human being had ever set foot upon. There were only a few ways up Denali. Most of it had never been walked upon by anyone. I was aiming the camera to capture extraordinary pictures of virgin territory, clickity-clicking as best I could. ABBA was singing loudly, and the plane was bouncing so hard that we had to duck our heads to keep from hitting the roof. Yet we all survived, and I am so *glad* to have taken that journey.

We landed and waited in a larger bus for some other people to return. A young man on a motorcycle drove up and asked if we needed anything while we waited. It might be half an hour before we left to return to the hotel. I asked if he would do me a favor: Go to the end of the runway where we had made a U-turn, use my camera, and take a picture of that little shack. He said, "Sure." About fifteen minutes later, he returned and said, "I'm so sorry. I looked up and down the little row of buildings. I couldn't find that written anywhere...."

I thanked him profusely and gave him a gratuity for his trouble. To you, dear reader, I swear it was real. I saw it. I blinked and blinked. I double and triple blinked to make sure. But can I *explain* it? No. Perhaps someday, when I pass away and meet Dad on the other side, he will be able to tell me where in the world that writing came from.

Finally, the day arrived when it was time to head home. As we were flying southward above central California, out the right side window I could see Yosemite National Park. There was Half Dome. There was El Capitan. My eyes began to mist up and tears rolled down my cheeks. I was flying *home* to beautiful San Diego, where I had lived for forty-one years. I was going home to so many friends. Home to where Wendy and little Jack would soon be returning from Kentucky—back once more to all the beautiful nature spots: the ocean, the mountains, and more varieties of birds and flowers than anywhere else in the United States (according to a lecture I had recently attended). Our home is a place others call a *resort.*

Gazing out the window, I was reminded once again wherein lies the real *gold* of life. Our deepest joys are in love and friendship, in beauty and nature (and pets!). All these treasures are free, gifts of the Creator. The *best* life has to offer has nothing to do with things purchased. Life's abundance is all around us every day, if we but open our hearts and minds to see it. All of it is *priceless* in value, comprising the *Ultimate* of blessings.

The porch

Above Denali

Making a new friend

On a salmon bake with cruise acquaintances from the east coast.

Holding a chunk of ice which had broken off the glacier
in the background, and floated ashore.

Cruising other islands aboard a smaller boat.

SOARING

This is the story of a wonderful happening involving a friend, myself and a delightful little bird. As a bit of background: Each day, I fill a hummingbird feeder with sweet red water. The feeder has been modified by taking out the little plugs in the center of the "flowers." It makes the holes bigger so that not only the hummingbirds can enjoy a cool drink. This feeder has become the "neighborhood bar" for even the larger birds. When spring arrives, I tape paper toweling to the top of the wooden porch railing. The birds peck at it, tearing off pieces with which to build their nests. I suspect it makes them nice and soft.

Now the wonderful story: Having just awakened on a Sunday morning, I walked into my second story apartment's living room, and noticed something unusual. There outside, on the floor of the wood-fenced balcony, were six little brown birds gathered around one tiny bird in the center. They all seemed concerned. The little one in the middle kept fluttering up a few inches, only to fall once again back to the floor.

Over and over this happened. I watched, not wishing to interfere with Mother Nature or frighten them. Perhaps they were trying to teach the little one to fly.

After about two minutes, when it appeared the little bird must be injured, I decided to venture out onto the porch to help. The caring companions all took flight as soon as the screen door opened. The little bird fluttered helplessly, trying to get away from me. Soon it was apparent what had happened. Outdoor green carpeting is put together with long thin fibers, apparently excellent "nest-building" material.

It seems this tiny bird had caught one of its feet in a long string of carpet fiber. The foot was all balled up and the string held it closely bound. The bird could not get free to fly away. The more it tugged and struggled, the tighter the string became.

It was easy to catch the bird in my hand and tear the opposite end of the fiber loose with my other hand. Then, in the left hand holding the bird, I secured the ankle of the bound foot between my little finger and the one next to it. My intention was to find scissors and cut the string loose. Entering the house, bird in hand, I tried to find the right instrument, all the while speaking softly, trying to let the little fellow (or girl) know I wouldn't harm it. Nothing found in the apartment seemed to suit the purpose, so I rang the bell of my neighbor, Laura, whose front door was but eight feet across from my own.

"Coincidentally," Laura was on vacation and her grown son Henok, a diabetic, was house sitting her little cat. We talked about the dilemma facing this tiny bird, all the while looking at it still in my hand. Who knows what the bird was thinking, being toted here and there in unfamiliar surroundings by big, tall "monster lady."

I considered a sewing needle, because the problem was the thinness of the string and how tightly it was bound. But a sewing needle would not be small enough to get to the "eye" of the knot which was very tiny and VERY tight. We stood at the kitchen sink and I sighed, "If only I had the right needle!" Henok offered, "*I have a needle!*" While he ran next door to fetch it, I found my magnifying glass. When he rushed back, in his hand was a brand new diabetic syringe, complete with needle. Henok held the magnifying glass while I tried to slip this wonderfully slim little needle into the eye of the knot, without poking the little bird's foot.

First try…*success!* The needle slipped in, I pulled it, the knot opened, and off came the fibrous thread that had bound the little bird's foot for so long. I gently stretched out its toes to make sure all was okay. The foot seemed just fine.

Then, out to the terrace…and like something out of a movie, we moved to the railing, my hand gently opened, and off soared the little one, a bird in flight; the most beautiful sight. The most *BEAUTIFUL* sight!

Sometimes our Creator lets us feel like some kind of "god" to these little ones by helping them. To me, it felt like a metaphor for the death experience. We struggle so at the end of life to hang on, and do everything in our human power to control our own ending. Ultimately, the Great Spirit comes with infinite compassion to untie the knot binding us to the experience of earthly suffering…and off we go, *SOARING!*

LOVE LETTER TO JACK

No book about miraculous stories from my life would be complete without a letter to you, Jack. On December 6, 2010, you turned five years old. How does one express to a special boy of five wishes for his life, which will still resonate as years progress—wishes which will have meaning when he is ten, a teenager, a young man, a person in love, a father, and an elderly gentleman?

One day, not too long ago, I began jotting down ideas to offer you as suggestions for happiness. These were gleaned from my own lifetime, and have served me well. Most were experienced personally, but some came from noticing other people's lives as well. They were first written as wishes, but now seem more like *axioms* (truths). It's easier to write them down as such, to express the ideas more succinctly. Please know these are merely suggestions. You must be the captain of your own ship of life, and set your *own* course! Here we go, off to read:

GRAMMY'S RECIPE FOR A HAPPY LIFE

GRATITUDE:
Savor (love that word!) *every* moment of living. If a good thing happens, it's good. If something is challenging, it's still good. You will learn something from it.
Each night as your head hits the pillow, say *Thank You* to Someone Greater than yourself (I like to say, "Thank you for Wednesday and all that was in it. Thank you for all the blessings of my lifetime to this very moment."). Appreciate all you have been given.

RELATIONS WITH OTHERS AND HAVING FUN:
Be a good friend. Treat everyone as you would like to be treated (the Golden Rule).
Be kind. Try never to hurt another either emotionally or physically. Both types of scars run deep.
Don't gossip. It wounds others. Choose compassion and tenderness over gossip and ridicule.
Try not to judge someone personally unless you have walked in another's shoes, and lived that person's life. Since none of us has, try never to judge or condemn.
If you like someone, show it.
If you disagree with someone, listen. It's okay to disagree without being disagreeable.
Hold friends dear. They are among the greatest treasures in life. Give to your friends unswerving loyalty and honesty.
"Show up" for your family and friends.
Learn how to lose. Don't be a bad sport, be a *good* one!

Find your greatest *riches* in experiences, people, relationships and nature, rather than in material things.

Practice "radical generosity" by sharing your time and substance.

One day I hope you will find the love of your life, someone to cherish, who will cherish you in return. Finding a loved one who is also your best friend in life is a winning combination.

Smile! It will make you and others feel good. Let all your smiles be *genuine.*

Even though you *will* grow up, always let your *inner child* express himself. Laugh and have fun. Feel things with all your heart. Be enthusiastic! Learn something new every day. Life is so exciting!

ETHICS:

Bring integrity, thoughtfulness, and joy to all you do.

Be open and honest. Hold fast to your own ethics.

Exhibit grace and self-assuredness wherever life takes you.

Speak out with authenticity and passion for what you believe.

Be straightforward and genuine. Folks who lie lead difficult and complicated lives, trying to remember to whom they told which lie. They lose track of *who* they really are. An honest person who is kind to others and tells the truth tends to rest comfortably on his or her pillow at night. It's easier to face the mirror in the morning.

A famous man of our time, Warren Buffett, claims one can build an honorable reputation over twenty years, yet have it destroyed in twenty minutes with unethical behavior.

The universe brings back to you that which you put out. Trust in that. Put out positives. Positive things will then happen to you in subsequent times, often unexpectedly—this principle is called karma.

Intention is the most important component of all of our actions. The inner desire which impels one to do something is more important than the action itself. Does one give money to a homeless person to show off his generosity in front of others, or does he do it from the authentic kindness of his heart?

Be totally yourself, who *you* wish to be. Then you will always be able to look in the mirror, and respect the person looking back.

TAKING CARE OF THE PHYSICAL:

Take good care of your body. Nourish it with healthy food and drink. It will then serve you well. Fill your plate with brightly colored natural foods. In our present day the advice is, "Make a rainbow on your plate."

Laugh often. When we smile, endorphins are released into the body. These natural substances relieve pain and depression, and give us a sense of well-being.

Never suppress anger. Doing so leads to physical illness. Talk things over with someone, or exercise to work out the anger. Remember, God will listen, too. You can speak to this Special Friend anytime.

Exercise moderately.

It's okay to cry sometimes. Tears are liquid love. It's *human* to cry.

Be self-reliant and your own best friend. Realize you are responsible for your own safety. Guard your physical body with firm decisions. Protecting yourself while engaging in sports, or choosing not to enter a car with an unsafe driver are two examples. Be smart. Do your best to stay out of harm's way.

Create a home environment that's your *haven*. Let it be a place of comfort, relaxation, and renewal—a place to venture out from each day, and return to for rest when the day is done. Be *thoughtful*. Enjoy your own quiet times of reflection.

CAREERS AND LEARNING:

Find an activity that makes you *come alive*—something that makes you *passionate* about living. Make that your career. It will give you joy, along with monetary compensation!

Realize that possessing an excessive amount of "stuff," and dwelling on material things, doesn't bring deep joy and lasting happiness.

Be justifiably proud *within yourself* for all of your accomplishments. Avoid being "full of yourself," and boasting to others.

Be open to new ideas that may be different from your own. Consider every side of an issue. Weigh all of your options, and then make a choice. This is a huge part of *wisdom*. Once you have made a decision, relax. Know you have made the best choice possible at that time, within those circumstances.

Keep your heart open. Cynicism can be a killer, both mentally and physically. Healthy skepticism is fine. It allows investigation of other possibilities.

Work hard, but not to the point of exhaustion. Don't become a "workaholic" to the exclusion of family, hobbies, periods of rest and reflection, etc. We all need balance in our lives. It keeps us sane.

Embrace learning. Be excited by new ideas. It will keep your mind involved, fill your days with meaning, and bring you joy.

LEAVING A LEGACY TO THE WORLD:

Leave the parts of the world and the people you visit each day better off than when you first arrived.

There exists a Force of love and compassion. When you connect with it, all the positives open up. Let your ego step aside. Try to be the greatest *good* you can be (service to others helps one feel fulfilled and happy).

Have good intentions toward others and the earth. Make this world a better place for Jack's having journeyed through it…and make your life your *message to the world*.

Let your life's purpose help perfect your love for others and the natural world.

As older generations pass away, "Old dreams find new wings," according to the lyrics of a bygone song. My biggest prayer is for world peace. I hope you will wish to carry on that ultimate dream. In future years, whether within families or among nations, sides will be able to sit down and talk, consider each other's opinions, and reach a consensus for resolution (a compromise beneficial to all)—without resorting to physical force or violence. Warlike violence will be thought of as barbaric, a relic of days long past.

On the wall of my bedroom is a little plaque containing impressions of your hand and foot when you were one year old. Ultimately, what *impression* will you leave upon the world? How will you impact the hearts of your friends? Will you use your best talents to uplift humanity? We shall see! You have already uplifted my life since the day you arrived, Jack, and you are only five!

FINALLY:

May you always love God, your ultimate Parent and Creator of everything and everyone—the One who is always by your side and will never desert you…not *ever*.

Believe your life is eternal. It *is*.

All who love you will have their own dreams for your life, but most important are *your own* dreams for how you wish your life experience to unfold. May all *your* dreams come true. If you are the best authentic "Jack" you can be, the world will be the richer for it.

Love, hugs, and kisses (too *many* to count),
Grammy

Jack had just turned four in December, 2009. Wendy took him to shop for a winter sweater. All by himself, he wandered over to a rack, and selected a black sport coat. "Can I have this, Mommy?"

Wendy replied, "Okay. We should get you a clip-on tie to go with it."

Jack's little friend, Carson, was also four years old. She was a blond "girly girl." Wendy was there the first time she saw Jack in his new outfit. Carson cooed, "Oooooh, Jack, you look soooooo Presidential!"

Who is the biggest of *all* these Superheroes?

A child's delight!

It's easy to hear the happy laughter….

IN THE COOL MIST OF YOSEMITE

On May 9, 1998, my loved one, Carol McKievick, made her transition. Since that time, her family had kept her ashes with the intention of one day laying them to rest in Yosemite, per her last request. The deposition of cremated remains is legally permitted in all of our national parks.

There is an expression used among many of my spiritual friends: "Everything in Divine Order." That's how it felt all during the trip to Yosemite with Carol's youngest brother Peter. Our mission was to place her ashes in the park she referred to as "My cathedral." Originally, her older brother Tom, and Carol's dear friend Marsha, planned to be on this trip as well—but that spring, their work schedules did not permit time away.

On Sunday, May 4, 2008, nearly ten years from the day of Carol's passing, Peter and I journeyed forth from San Diego at 7:00 a.m. We had lots of beautiful CDs along, which made the journey of nine hours very pleasurable. Peter was a great traveling companion. We learned this travel tip: Going through Los Angeles at about 10:00 a.m. on a Sunday, and coming back through LA at 2:00 p.m. on a Wednesday, are great ways to avoid the usual bumper to bumper traffic.

In Yosemite, we stayed at a beautiful hotel about two miles outside of the park's boundary. It had a "Four Diamond" AAA recommendation, so I'm sure Carol was pleased. Having spent her Chicago childhood in very humble surroundings, she loved to stay in "nothing less than a Three Diamond."

On Monday morning, we set out to complete our mission. We decided to deposit Carol's ashes in Yosemite Falls, which were thundering and very full. She always suggested that the best months to visit the park were April and May. One should always call ahead to see how much water is in the falls, because the volume of water depends upon the amount of snowfall the previous winter. We were very fortunate this year with comfortable temperatures, no mosquitoes, and water gushing from every fall. Upper Yosemite Fall was very *robust* with an abundance of water. It cascaded in a straight line into Lower Yosemite Fall. We chose the cross bridge at the base of this lower waterfall, where the noise was thunderous and the mist mighty. There was a great cool wind emitting from the mist blowing outward across the bridge—a perfect place to stand if one didn't wish the ashes to wind up on a fellow tourist.

We were strolling halfway up the trail to the falls, when I noticed there were only three pictures left in the camera. It seemed wise to insert a new roll of film at that moment. Peter could empty the ashes, and I would be off to the side, recording the moment for Tom and Marsha. My resolve was to not "mess up" by running out of film at the crucial moment. After removing the film, I inserted a new one and advanced it—but an "E" (error) appeared in the window of the camera. After a few more attempts, the "E" remained. Then, inside the camera, we spotted a little piece of what looked like old film. We tried and tried to remove it, but to no avail. We started asking passers-by if they might have a pair of tweezers or a pocket knife. Finally, a wonderful couple, Denis and Lisa, came by with their two kids. Denis pulled out a Swiss Army sort of knife which included a perfect pair of tweezers. He tried valiantly to fix the problem, but eventually, we all realized the camera was broken. Peter and I shared with them the reason the pictures were so important to us. Lisa then offered, "Why don't *we* take your pictures, and e-mail them to you when we get home?" Yay!

Off we all journeyed to the base of Lower Yosemite Fall. Peter expressed a few second thoughts because there were so many kids running around on the bridge. It was understandable how he felt—not much of a setting for a solemn, quiet ceremony. Given his hesitation, I offered to be the one to open the bag of ashes into the wind. We did it standing together, while kind-hearted Denis snapped away. Peter emptied the last remaining ashes with a final shake, making sure they had all escaped into the wind. Denis took one last picture of the two of us standing on the bridge in front of the falls. Before parting, we exchanged e-mail addresses and phone numbers with Denis and Lisa. It was so kind of them to use precious moments of their own vacation to help perfect strangers.

Peter and I then found a wooden bench next to the falls. We read Tom's Bible verses aloud. Peter offered his own silent prayer. I said one audibly, basically saying to the Creator that, "These are the last earthly remains of Your precious child, Carol. You know her best and love her best. We thank You that we had the privilege of sharing in her life while she was here on earth." I don't remember the exact words, but those were the basic sentiments of the prayer. Then we sat in silence for a while. With people all around, we were lost in our own private thoughts. Tears came gently and quietly. Ten years had come and gone. It was beautifully comforting to just sit there and feel the cool mist and wind, listening to the thunder and power of the falls. After a while, we journeyed back down the trail, mission accomplished.

Maybe the camera breaking was to once again put things in Divine Order. My daughter Wendy had been urging me to get a digital camera. Perhaps Carol wanted both of us in those pictures. If I had taken them, Peter would have been standing there alone.

One day, we had lunch in the Ahwahnee Hotel dining room. There were two waiters named Paul whom I met in the space of ten minutes, so I thought maybe my dad Paul, who had passed away in 2000, was "along" on this adventure. Also, on the last day at an outdoor café, a huge blue jay lit on a table not far from where we were standing, and just stayed and stayed, not flying off or even seeming afraid. My dad used to feed a blue jay in his backyard. The jay would stand on the edge of his hand, and choose morsels of food from his palm. That was another *sign* I thought Dad might be along. We strolled inside and outside the Ahwahnee, so Peter could absorb the whole ambiance of Carol's favorite hotel.

Peter had never been to Yosemite before. I like to think it pleased Carol to know her youngest brother's first experience entailed seeing the park with all of its waterfalls so abundantly full.

We then journeyed higher to Glacier Point, which offered views of so many famous parts of the valley—Half Dome, the Merced River, Vernal Falls, Nevada Falls, and the Ahwahnee Hotel below us. There was still snow on the ground at that elevation. Peter picked up a handful and I did likewise, unable to resist taking a bite...it wasn't yellow!

As we drove back through the park entrance one day at the ranger station, songwriter Neil Sedaka was on a CD singing a song he originally wrote for the Captain and Tennille, *Love Will Keep Us Together*. This is difficult to describe, but we had to turn right at two stop signs about 20 feet apart. Just as I stepped on the brake at each sign, Neil said the word STOP. Picture it: "STOP! 'Cause I really love you" (20 feet later) "STOP! I been thinkin' of you." These were perfectly in sync, one right after the other. I turned to Peter and asked, "Did you see what just happened?" Amazing synchronicity.

The hotel left a copy of *USA Today* outside each of our doors every morning. The last morning's newspaper contained a *huge* article about trapping, neutering and releasing feral cats. It reflected just the kind of work Carol loved to do with the Feral Cat Coalition in San Diego. It was a pretty narrow window of time to get that article in during the three days we were in Yosemite...more Divine Order?

On our final morning, we drove out of the park and were making our way down the mountain. In a little town, on the right side of the road, we spotted a small McDonald's restaurant. We hadn't had breakfast, so stopped to pick up a bite to eat along the way. As we were waiting inside for our order, a woman walked through the door and exclaimed, "Well, look who's here!" It was Lisa, the wife of Denis, who had taken our photos at the falls. This chance meeting occurred two days after the picture taking. Imagine how many people visit Yosemite! If either of our parties had been five minutes earlier or later, we would not have met up again. *More synchronicity!*

We stopped for lunch that same day at a restaurant in Santa Ana. Over the sound system, while Peter visited the restroom, came the song *My Heart Will Go On*. It's a song I've identified with Carol ever since her passing. It comes into my head at least a couple of times a week, whether I'm thinking of her or not. It just seems to validate that life does go on and on. Had Peter been there with the two of us conversing, I might not have noticed the soft music playing in the background.

Finally, on Mother's Day, May 11, 2008, four days after our return: I was driving south on highway I-15, after visiting with my daughter Wendy, when in front of me appeared a green Passat with the license plate *LEANLFT*. Many years before, Carol had spoken fondly of this license, which belonged to her friend, Marsha. It was such a clever plate espousing liberal ideals, I never forgot it. Surely this must be Marsha, whom I hadn't seen in person for years and years. I called her the following morning at work and, sure enough, it *was* her!

Some people call these things *coincidences*. I love the book, *When God Winks: How the Power of Coincidence Guides Your Life* by SQuire Rushnell (yes, it is spelled with a capital Q). Maybe someday, when Marsha and I cross over, Carol will explain this special rendezvous to us. With all the cars on the freeway, if we had been even ten seconds apart at that speed, this encounter would not have occurred. Marsha was supposed to be on the ashes trip, per the planning we had done years before. Though we had spoken on the phone, I had not seen her for ten years. I think Carol was saying "Hello" to her through this Divine appointment.

Thank you, Dear Creator, and thank you, Carol. Love *does* go on and on in *Divine Order*.

Postscript:

On Fridays at noon, I attend a singing class of about 15 people. Some of us enrolled there are also writers. Lois, one of the class members, gave me a wonderful piece she had written about her recent trip to Warren Buffet's Berkshire/Hathaway stockholders' meeting in Omaha, Nebraska, which she knew was my hometown. In return, I had given her this latest writing about Yosemite. One week after receiving it, she leaned over in class and whispered, "Marsha with the *LEANLFT* license plate is in my Jazzercise class." I later called Marsha, who quickly verified that she did indeed know Lois.

Just think of the precise planning for the freeway encounter to have occurred *and* the remote probability that in such a small group of singers, one of them would know Marsha! All of the events in this entire story occurred within the first 23 days of May, 2008.

How do we wrap our thoughts around the complexity of intricate planning by unseen Sources that *orchestrate* these events, which occur with so much synchronicity? If I had been born in any town other than Omaha, chances are that Lois would not have thought to give me her Berkshire/Hathaway piece.

The Creator, in His/Her infinite wisdom, leaves us no room to label these occurrences as anything but uncanny, unexplainable *miracles*.

Upper Yosemite Fall, gushing!

On the trail to Upper and Lower Yosemite Falls

FOR YOU, JAN

A dear friend of mine who lives in Arizona is also named Janet. She goes by the name Jan, and spent her earliest years in New England. Two women in the *maturing* time of life, we love to share frequent correspondence. She writes beautifully descriptive letters, and is a tremendously optimistic person. Life recently has been challenging for Jan and her wonderful husband Bob—circumstances which have led to my wishing them well in thoughts and prayers.

On the morning of August 23, 2010, while out driving on errands, I was listening to a CD by Anne Murray entitled, *Croonin'*. One of the most beautiful cuts on the album, *Old Cape Cod*, prompted the idea, "I'll bet Jan would love this CD. I must send it to her."

Having just finished that thought, I rolled to a stop behind a car at a red light. There on the license plate was *4UJAN C*. I took it as a "sign," and subsequently mailed the CD to Arizona. During that time in our lives, it's fun to think the "C" might have stood for CD!

Had I arrived thirty seconds earlier or later, or even been in another lane (there were three on that side of the road), I would have missed seeing this uniquely unusual license plate. There was barely time to take a single breath between the moment of the finished thought and the sighting of the license plate. Perhaps the vehicle had been an earlier gift to a person named Jan.

Was this happening mere *coincidence?* Not likely. I choose to believe instead that none of us is journeying through life alone. There are unseen beneficent and beautiful presences helping us along, offering us optimism, giving us hope and blessings every single day, if we but open our eyes to see.

Jan and Bob with their granddaughters, Clara (left) and Alicia.

OH, TO BE FOREVER FIVE

I remember being all of five, feeling so very much *alive*. Emotions were boiled down to their essence: Love, sorrow, joy, anger; just pure happy or sad, glad or mad.

And curiosity! I pondered every new thing by touch, smell, sight, sound and taste. My eyes drank it in with an unquenchable thirst. Did it *bounce* when I dropped it? Was it squishy or hard? What *shape* was it? What color was it on the *inside?* What did it *say* to me when I stared at it from every which way? Each newly discovered surprise was "neat." Every day held the promise of learning something new. I saw blue sky and white clouds in the middle of a puddle after a rain. I jumped in. Imagine, jumping *into* the sky!

Death at five was merely a clutching of the stomach, a fall to the ground, a tumble down a hill—jumping up once again, after just a moment of *still*. My finger took aim at a friend peeking out from a tree, *"Bam!* Take that! You'll never catch *me!"*

If restlessness visited playtime at home, escape was in the garage. I'd bolt out the front door, hop onto my bike and go! Should tears follow sadness in five's busy days, the wind on my face swiftly blew them away—and each hurt was forgotten by the end of the day.

I was responsible for no one's feelings but my own. When I laughed, it came from a place way down deep inside. Seeing the twinkle in my eyes at such a happy moment, anyone present might also smile with delight. Joy is infectious. A child makes other people happy…effortlessly.

It has been said, "One must become as a child to enter the kingdom of heaven." An authentic person can be real and honest with feelings, experience the greatest of joys, and also admit to pain and sadness. If ever I was lonely back then, no problem. I'd meander down the street to find a buddy who could play. If I was mad at someone, they probably deserved it, because they had done "something mean."

Tucked in bed with me at night was a happy kind of tired. It felt so warm and good to know Mom and Dad, chatting in the living room, would keep everything safe until morning.

The next time I have a birthday, do me a favor. Please forget all those candles… Just light five.

Mom and me (age 5)

HEROES

Each of us has, in our own life, one or more persons who set the standard as honored role models. When we think of them, we inevitably smile. It's a smile born of admiration. For me, the word *heroes* personifies my maternal grandparents. (My dad's parents had already passed on by the time I was born. Dad shared how wonderful they were. I wish I could have met them in person).

Alex and Ines Nelson, my mother's parents, traced their immediate ancestry back to Sweden and Scotland, respectively. Their lives came together about 1903, or so.

The date is a "guesstimate." Their first child, Edward, was born in 1905. When Grandma was a child on the Nebraska prairie, her family lived in a little sod house, and traded with a nearby Native American tribe. As a young man, Grandpa served in the U. S. Navy, traveling to the Far East. All of the early history of these two special people is in other places of record. These are some of my own personal memories of special times spent with Grandma and Grandpa.

Saturdays were magical. Why? Because on that day, Mom and I would drive from the suburbs of Omaha, Nebraska to 4006 No. 42nd Street, Grandma and Grandpa's place. Many years before, Grandpa had built a two-story home, which eventually housed their family of six children. It rested on a nice big plot of land, with room for a large vegetable garden and compost pile, plus space to raise their own chickens. There were fruit trees along the side and back of the house, and a big walnut tree in the front yard.

On Saturdays, we would first climb the wide wooden steps of their huge front porch, complete with its roomy, beckoning swing. In spring and summer, there was always the delicious aroma of freshly baked pies wafting out the screen door. Grandma was in the kitchen. It seemed Grandma was *always* in the kitchen. The cellar was filled with jars of her canned fruits, vegetables and pickles. Grandma and Grandpa didn't have a lot of money, but their home always felt like a place of great *abundance* in all things that mattered.

I never heard either of them raise their voice in anger, or use a curse word. Everything seemed to flow along with an easy, gentle rhythm, with Grandma cooking and looking after everyone (utilizing the washing machine and wringer in the basement, clothesline in the backyard, and a darning egg for mending the holes in Grandpa's socks). Grandpa was involved with his day job, gardening (planting and harvesting organically grown foods for their delicious family meals), and fixing whatever needed fixing throughout the house and property. About Grandpa: He was a tradesman, and at one point repaired elevators. All of his jobs provided a good living wage for the family. My earliest memory of him is from the age of five. We arrived one Saturday, and noticed Grandpa standing by the side of the house. He was adding a new coat of white paint.

"Would you like to help me paint the house?"

Never having done such a thing, I felt totally inadequate. Grandpa was about to discover that his little granddaughter was shy and had no talent, especially in things as complex as painting houses.

"I don't know how, Grandpa."

"It's easy. Here, I'll show you. You just dip the brush in the can about halfway, remove the excess paint by touching it on the lip of the can, then brush the paint sideways, all in the same direction."

In an instant, the two of us were happily painting away. My insecurity, self-doubt and shyness had disappeared. He sure knew how to build a kid's self esteem. Later, upon entering the house, I proudly proclaimed to Mom, "I've been out helping Grandpa paint the house!"

Grandpa always had his pocket knife handy. He would saunter into the living room carrying a piece of fresh fruit. If it was an apple, he would sit in his big easy chair, slice off a piece with his knife and offer a bite to share. To a little kid, his demeanor was awesome; his smile, his easy confidence, his eagerness to share, and his gentle manliness.

During a semester at the University of Nebraska, I visited Grandma and Grandpa one weekend. They put me up in their own front bedroom, the one where Grandma had given birth so many times. They chose to sleep on the enclosed back porch those two nights. I was just drifting off to sleep when I heard my elderly grandfather singing softly to Grandma, "I love you truly, truly dear...." There in the darkness, all by myself, I couldn't help but smile, listening to the *tenderness* of all that love, which had endured for so many years.

While visiting them, I made a book for my mom entitled *On A Sunday Afternoon*. I was studying black and white photography in college at the time, and took candid shots of Grandma and Grandpa when they weren't aware I was taking their picture. Thus, the relaxed nature of their wonderful home is conveyed with no one posing. I love looking through it all these years later. It's like being there once more, and feeling the gentle love in their home all over again.

I think when all of her relatives revisit Grandma in our minds, what we remember most is her food, the way she *took care* of everyone by feeding us all the time. Her dining room table for lunch or dinner was always set the same way: a container of spoons, salt and pepper shakers, a saucer with a stick of butter, and a jar of her pickles. All these necessary extras would be in the middle. At each place, there was a plate, paper napkin and silverware. A piece of pie was *already* next to your plate when you sat down to begin the meal!

On another visit during college, I sat in Grandma's dining room one afternoon while she was ironing. We spoke of many things. I asked if she would share her apple pie recipe, so I could write it down. She seemed bemused, and explained that she just cooked by instinct. She went on to say that for the crust you use a fistful of lard. "You'd probably call it Crisco. Maybe about a cup." Spoonfuls of dry tapioca were used to thicken a fruit pie, so the juices wouldn't get too runny. All these years later, I can still see us having that wonderful chat. Grandma then brought a shoebox full of old photos down from the attic. While looking through the pictures, I remarked what a treasure they were.

"Would you like to *have* them someday?"

"Oh, *yes!*"

"Well, just write on the top cover of the box, 'Give to Janet.'"

Years after Grandma passed away, my aunt Virdeen came to California for a visit, and mentioned she had something for me. It was the shoebox. What a beautiful *gift* from Grandma!

For years and years and years, Grandma used to keep a pad of paper and a pencil next to her radio. Every single weekday, she made sure she was home to catch a radio program called *The Grocery Boy*. Its host would announce a dollar amount, and then call someone at random out of the phone book. If the listener correctly gave the amount, he or she would receive that sum of money in groceries. Grandma would write down the figure in hopes of being called. She did this for many many years, but her phone didn't ring. She never lost hope.

When I was a freshman at college in California, I missed Grandma, and wished to do something to make her happy. I wrote a letter to *The Grocery Boy*, informing the host of how faithful she had been to his program. I asked if he could bend the rules just a little. I assured him that no matter what day he called, she would be there with the right answer. A little time went by. Then came a happy letter from Grandma saying that she had *won* the grocery prize! I never did tell her how that came about. Her diligence over all those years deserved to be its own reward.

Finally, July Fourth. Every year, the big backyard would be set up with picnic tables, and nearby wash tubs, filled with whole watermelons and large chunks of ice. We grandkids would take turns churning homemade ice cream. Grandma, despite her very modest income, would cook for everyone. She fried all the chicken, prepared side dishes from their garden, and of course, made all the pies. Her daughter Phyllis's family (last name Myers) came from as far away as California back to the family home in Omaha. There were about thirty of us altogether.

Each Independence Day, the atmosphere was filled with lots of laughter and visiting, sharing the latest news from each of our families. Then sunset came. We all walked a few blocks up the street to Fontenelle Park, and spread blankets to watch the fireworks with other families. I've spoken of these July Fourth holidays with several relatives over the years. We always remember them with great fondness—All that hospitality, and all that love, from the perfect host and hostess, who did not have much financial abundance, but had so much to *give*.

My grandparents worked very hard all their lives to provide for the family they loved. They endured many hardships. I've chosen to leave those out in this writing, except for this next, which deeply touched my heart. The six children of Ines and Alex were named (in birth order) Edward, Phyllis, Rena, Virdeen, Orville and Stella. My mother Rena shared that Stella was the "prettiest" of all the girls. She passed away in her mother's arms at the age of two, while my own mother looked on. It was a sudden death, a bit of a mystery, without even time to summon a doctor. There was a feeling of devastation in their whole family, because they all loved her so. My grandparents were always a couple with great faith in God. I admire both of them tremendously for persevering through this untimely personal tragedy.

So here's to the *heroes*. Thank you both for giving all of us who knew you a wonderful example of everything important in life: a love of God and family, devotion to each other, honesty in your lives and in your labors, good humor, delicious food…and the care given to every single one of us with so much constancy. You were always there, always present, always giving, always loving…never *ever* to be forgotten.

Grandpa and Grandma

Grandma's welcoming dinner table

LEONARD BERNSTEIN

It was Easter Week, 1987. Being a single working mother, every year I would put aside $1,500—so that my daughter Wendy and I could vacation in some exciting new place. This particular year, we decided to explore New York City. My good friend, Carol Stuchfield from Nottingham, England, agreed to fly to Manhattan to join us. We, in turn, would fly from San Diego. It was sort of a mutual "meeting in the middle," and would be 12-year-old Wendy's first trip to New York City.

We all shared a suite at the Beverly Hotel, across the street from the Waldorf Astoria. The first evening, we ventured out to the Waldorf's first-floor lounge. There the three of us enjoyed beverages, while listening to a wonderful singer and pianist, Rich Siegel. He was "tickling the ivories" on the piano once owned by composer Cole Porter, who years before had maintained an apartment at the Waldorf. After he passed away, they moved the piano from his residence upstairs down to the lounge. During a break in the performance, while standing beside it, we could still see the rings left by his martini glasses so many years before.

Some of the fun of New York City was dining in small cafes. We enjoyed breakfast at a popular deli in the neighborhood. Its walls boasted photos of famous motion picture and television stars. One day, we saw a movie filming on the street. There was Steve Martin shooting a scene! A fellow came walking toward us and asked, "Okay, which of you extras hasn't been paid yet?" Honest to a fault, we scurried away, unaware that we had been standing in a crowd of extras. Gee, I wonder how much each of them earned? We also did the usual things: the Statue of Liberty, the Empire State Building, Central Park, Times Square, plus other points of interest. What fun!

On one of the seven days, Carol traveled south to visit an old friend in Washington, D. C. Wendy and I were left with a whole day and evening to ourselves. Thinking it might be fun to see a show, we took a cab downtown to the half-price ticket booth outlet. Nearly every musical offered we had seen before, having used our season tickets to the Starlight Bowl in San Diego. We noticed the New York Philharmonic was playing symphonic music by Schubert that very night at Lincoln Center. Leonard Bernstein was conducting! I phoned the box office. The woman who answered suggested, "How about the seventh row center? It's Passover, and many of our Jewish patrons will not be attending." Wendy, just entering her teens, had never been to a symphony. *Yes!* We would *love* to have those tickets!

That night, donning our best bib and tucker, we journeyed by cab to Lincoln Center. The seats were perfect. We were able to see maestro Bernstein, full of excitement, leaping at least a foot off the podium (this was three and a half years or so before he passed away in October 1990 at the age of 72). He seemed filled with enthusiastic passion for the music. We could see clearly the facial expressions of the musicians as they interacted with him. How they seemed to delight in the gusto of his fiery exuberance!

During intermission, we glanced through the program. In small print was an invitation to the second floor for anyone wishing to meet the artists following the performance. Wendy and I were both excited at the prospect of meeting Leonard Bernstein in person. Following the concert, we made our way upstairs. Soon a guard appeared to the few hundred gathered there. He announced with regret that Mr. Bernstein was very tired. He would not be able to see anyone. There was a huge collective sigh. People began descending the stairs toward the exit doors.

I suggested to Wendy that we ought to leave the great conductor a note of thanks and appreciation, because this was her first symphony experience. I scribbled a note on a piece of paper, folded it, and asked the guard if he would please give it to Mr. Bernstein. He looked up and down the hallway. No one was in sight. "Oh, it's okay," he smiled, "Why don't you just go on ahead to his dressing room?" He cordially opened a door, and directed us down a long hallway.

We soon arrived at another doorway. It was standing open. Inside, facing us, sat the musical legend, relaxing on a wooden chair, his knees on either side of a small round table in front of him. Atop the table was a large round ashtray filled with cigarette butts. He was wearing a maroon smoking jacket, and looked totally exhausted. A few friends were in the room with him. We timidly approached. I remember saying hello to Mr. Bernstein, then introducing myself and Wendy. I shared that we were from San Diego, and that this was my daughter's first symphonic experience. We expressed appreciation for the opportunity to meet him in person.

He looked up, smiled and loudly said to Wendy, "Your *first* time? What a hell of a way to begin!" I asked if I might take a picture of the two of them. He put one hand on each knee and began to rise.

I offered, "No, please, don't get up. Wendy can just kneel down beside you." Thus was born one of my favorite pictures of Wendy, with a very kindhearted gentleman who couldn't have been more gracious. Knowing how tired he was, we began to make a quick exit. We thanked him profusely. He reached out and shook Wendy's hand. Then he shook mine and said, "Thank you for coming." I nodded and began to withdraw my hand. He grabbed it again very firmly, looked into my eyes and said, "Really...*thank you.*"

I thought about that special moment again and again from time to time over the years that followed. It was during the late 1950s, and in subsequent years, that Leonard Bernstein would sponsor programs for school children in New York City. These eventually made their way to nationwide television. The series entailed introducing young children to the wonders of classical music, and also explaining all the orchestral instruments. He encouraged them to attend concerts with their parents. Many performances were offered free to disadvantaged children. He was a pioneer in early childhood classical music education.

I think those earlier experiences led to the enthusiasm in his final handshake. He had delighted a *child* once again, providing the gift of her *first* symphonic experience; just as he had done for other countless children years before.

Thank YOU to the wonderful guard. With his kindness, he opened the door to a magical memory on one very special springtime evening in New York City.

Wendy and Leonard Bernstein

STRENGTH TO POWER

Life sometimes presents us with special unforeseen opportunities. One such occurrence happened following a phone call from a friend in the late 1990s. She was a practicing psychologist and professor of psychology at a university in the San Diego area. She asked if I would like to attend a presentation before a gathering of psychology students. The speaker would be a convicted criminal, currently serving a lengthy prison sentence. The small forum seated about 150, and was shaped in a semicircle, with seats gradated upward. My folding chair was at the top, behind the last row of students.

All was silent as a young man, handcuffed at the waist, and wearing ankle chains, was led in by guards, and seated on a chair facing the students. He was small of stature, twenty-four years old, with light brown hair and piercing blue eyes (picture actor Paul Newman's eyes, ladies). His voice was steady, though soft-spoken. Slightly trembling, he recounted the story of his life, including specific circumstances that led to his imprisonment.

It seems he had been abused as a small child. Growing up, he realized that visiting the gym often was of great importance. Not very tall, he thought it necessary to become "powerful" physically to protect himself from harm. Building a strong physique became the paramount objective in his life.

At long last, he achieved his goal. Now he would have dominance over others— the weak, the defenseless, and the smallest in society, the children. No longer a helpless little boy, the tables had been turned, all in his favor.

Physical power and its importance became the subject of the majority of his talk. I took no notes, but just kept searching his eyes and his demeanor. There were surprising discoveries in those moments. I sensed a person with goodness inside, with gentleness perhaps seldom expressed—and those eyes, the color of ocean and sky, clear and shining.

Eventually, he finished and was escorted out. The students began to disperse. I wished to do *something* to help him. He was so young with his whole life before him. He faced many more years in prison. Arriving back home, I decided one thing I could do would be to write him a letter. It began by explaining that I would not say if I was a man or woman, because it didn't really matter (actually, I didn't wish to reveal that, because he might have prejudices from his past about one or the other). In the remainder of the letter, I began to describe (from my own perspective) *who* seemed to be sitting there in front of the students. I had observed goodness and gentleness way down deep inside, with the potential to be genuinely influential in the world, in a very positive way.

I shared with him that, over many years, I had discovered a very *different* kind of *power*, something apart from the physical. The letter went on to encourage him to quietly sit down with another person. During their conversation, he might try to share with that individual qualities he admired about him or her. Perhaps he or she never recognized some of these positive, inherent traits. Such a gesture on his part would be using *positive power*, which entails the ability to enlighten and transform someone else's whole existence. It might change for the better the remainder of someone's life, and had nothing to do with the *physical*.

Later, I presented this letter to the professor, who forwarded it to the prison authority. It was delivered to the young man. A few weeks later, there was another phone call from the psychologist. She had been contacted by the leader of a support group for prisoners. He informed her that the young man had opened the letter and read it. He kept it in his back pocket. From time to time, he would take it out, unfold it, and study it. This happened over and over again. Eventually, he offered to read it to the circle of men in his support group. As he finished, the leader reported, these *hardened* criminals had tears in their eyes. Evidently what the letter writer had seen in this one young man, each of the others had recognized in himself.

If people in circumstances of prison confinement can have their hearts touched in a tender way, maybe there is hope for the future. If we can find a way to heal the victims of child abuse, to heal what that early experience does to a child's self esteem, perhaps we will have far fewer occurrences of abuse…and, at some point down the road, no more victims at all.

Does this seem an *impossible dream?* Dreams are worth pursuing with all due diligence and determination, especially *this* one—a dream for our children.

THERE IS A PLACE

There is a place on this beautiful planet where each of us finds pure tranquility, away from the *busyness* and challenges of life—a place which feels as if the Creator bestowed a special *kiss* upon the earth. You have yours, and I have mine.

Come along with me, and sit atop a grassy cliff overlooking the blue Pacific Ocean. You can see so far to the horizon, that it seems as if the very curvature of the earth is visible. White gulls soar high above, and often land at your feet, begging for a morsel of whatever you have on hand. Pelicans glide overhead in perfect V formations, following the coastline. Sometimes they number ten or less, but often, there are fourteen to forty of them. Beautiful. On occasion, they fly much lower, gliding only a few feet above the ocean waves.

If you've brought a sack filled with unsalted raw peanuts in the shell, little squirrels will scamper up close enough for you to feed them.

The air is pristine due to westerly sea breezes, and refreshes like a magical elixir. Whenever I feel a cold or flu coming on, I go to this nurturing spot and, voila! Upon arriving back home, the symptoms are gone. Once I was privileged to meet a woman who owns a home just across the street from this wondrous place. She informed me that it's a vortex of energy, much like Sedona, Arizona. It's a special healing site, and makes folks feel so *good* (if they can bear to put their cell phones and BlackBerries away, and willingly lose themselves in appreciation of the natural world). The ocean also works its magic if there is a special challenge presenting itself in life; something causing stress and the ponderous, nervous thoughts it can bring. It's gently *freeing* to enjoy an hour or more of just relaxing, watching the beautiful white-capped waves crash against the sandy shore.

Problems seem much smaller when compared to the majesty of the boundless beauties of nature; the ocean, brisk breezes, brightly colored flowers, and inquisitive birds and squirrels—and dogs! Many people walk their dogs along this grassy cliff top. Often one will approach, tail wagging, eager to make your acquaintance. It's fun to ask the owner the pet's name and how old it is, along with other little tidbits of information. Meanwhile, there's the added bonus of getting to pet the friendly doggy or pup.

On days when the waves are strong, there are board surfers, body boarders and body surfers having a *swell* time riding them. You might also see folks snorkeling. Occasionally, the little black olive-colored head of a seal will pop up from waves nearest the shore. Further out to sea, during the January to March migration of gray whales, you can observe these magnificent huge mammals breaching and crashing down sideways—or they might spout water from their blowholes while surfacing for huge gulps of air. Binoculars come in handy at such times.

People come from all over the world to see this unique spot while visiting San Diego. Often, while strolling the sidewalks meandering up and down the coastline, you'll hear people in front of or behind you, excitedly chatting away in various languages and dialects.

If you journey along the coast north of this beautiful site, eventually you'll come to a tall lifeguard tower. In front of the tower, in a protected sandy cove, is a seal rookery. Years ago, mother seals came to this protected place, deciding it was an ideal place to give birth and raise their young. Between February and June, mother and baby seals in large numbers can be seen relaxing; sleeping on the warm sand, or swimming in the protected waters. Tourists from the United States and foreign countries enjoy watching the placid nature of such domesticity from atop brick walls surrounding the cove's nursery. It's a memorable and rewarding experience, never to be forgotten.

I first saw this special cliff in 1965, while visiting San Diego in search of employment. It took but one glimpse of the spectacular panorama for me to promise myself, "I am never leaving." Writing this in 2010, I'm happy to say that I never have. Every day at the ocean is unique. The color of the water is unpredictable—the waves may be large and crashing, or glassy and small. Wildlife are doing their own thing, the number of seagulls present often depending upon the number of people picnicking on the grass, willing to share their tidbits of food. On a cold, gray day, there may be only three or four people along the entire length of the cliff. The calm serenity of sitting, observing and listening to the sounds of the natural world is a treat unto itself, even on the coldest of days.

I considered relating some of the miracle stories encountered at this special place. But as I began listing them, there were just too many during the last forty-five years. They themselves could fill a book. It would be more meaningful for you to have your own special experiences, should you choose to visit this unnamed, beautiful spot. It has become, in my life, a cathedral of nature. Here one feels so near the essence and power of Creation. Yes, there is a place—my favorite haven in all the world.

Directions:

If you visit the San Diego area, find La Jolla Cove on a map, or simply by asking directions. The Cove is a grassy park on a cliff top next to the ocean, and is lovely to explore in its own right. Venture south, casually strolling along the coastline sidewalk, or driving along the adjacent road. You'll come to the large lifeguard tower on your right, and hopefully observe seals resting in front of it. Continue south along the cliffs. Eventually you will come to a fork in the road. In the center of the fork sits a single house. The grassy cliff is directly across the street from this home. Relax, and drink in the colors and sounds of the Pacific coast. Breathe deeply of the ocean air. Take what you will from this wonderful site. It offers much, and asks nothing in return. It's a place where Mother Nature offers her unconditional love to all….

Three species, all getting along, enjoying a wonderful day by the ocean.

In my favorite spot, with a little friend.

WHERE DO THEY COME FROM?

Every person on earth has a certain talent that just comes easily. How about you? Perhaps there is something you love to do that seems as natural as breathing. Others may find that same task quite challenging. Each of us has certain *given* abilities.

In considering our own lives, we may wonder *where* talent comes from. Some of these skills seem to have been born in us. From a very young age, special aptitudes are apparent.

In my own life, there is one talent that doesn't seem to be genetically inherited. To my knowledge, nobody else in the family has a history of it. That ability is drawing.

When I was in college, electives could be chosen outside of one's major course of study. There in the catalog was *Drawing Logic 001*. Like many people, my own drawing experience, while growing up, had been with stick figures. I never had a course in high school that involved sketching. I remember thinking, "Hey, that might be fun, learning how to draw!"

Our class was provided large easels with pads of paper (measuring about 24 x 36 inches) clipped to them. The medium was black charcoal. The easels were arranged in a large circle, inside which were displayed still lifes and live models. During the hour, the instructor would make his way around the circle, strolling behind us, and stopping at each easel to provide constructive criticism.

As luck would have it, seated next to me was a very talented young man who seemed skilled beyond his years. His sketches were so detailed that they resembled photographs. The professor would stop and give him negative criticism, telling him he was *rendering* too much (making things look too realistic). Week after week, he pounded this student with unflattering remarks. I didn't understand it. To me, the young man was a genius.

When our teacher came to my easel, he spoke very gently, and his remarks were always brief. Then, he would move on. I assumed he recognized me as a novice to the art experience. He was just being tolerant and kind.

We were asked to purchase blank sketch books. During our time away from the classroom, we were to find various subjects to draw, eventually turning our books in to the instructor for his review.

When he returned the sketch books, he privately said that "some" of mine were very interesting. I remember him asking, "Didn't you say you've never had a drawing class?" Being very embarrassed, I just nodded. I thought he was inferring, "Why in the world are you in *this* class of art students?" He gave me an assignment. The professor asked me to visit the local museum and draw from some of the "masters," artists famous in history. He said to use a pen with India ink. Unlike charcoal, which could be erased and corrected, using black ink meant once a line was put on the paper, it would be permanent.

At the time, I felt terrible. Other members of the class did not have to do this extra work. I assumed my work was vastly inferior to that of the other students. This must be an attempt to bring me up to speed.

The above events happened in my early twenties. I put the artwork away, and forgot about it. Drawing, with my inherent lack of skill, did not seem a field worth pursuing.

On Christmas Eve of 2000, at age 55, I received a computer from my daughter Wendy. During that same year, I rediscovered some of this old artwork. With the new technology, it was possible to compare the original drawings of the masters with my own, copied so carefully in India ink years before. I also found my sketch book containing the charcoal drawings.

Encountering memories of more than thirty years before was painful, but now it was possible to look at the drawings with a new pair of eyes. Wonder of wonders, rather than seeing inferiority in my work, I began to realize our professor might have been seeing *promise*.

In my early twenties, I was dating a fellow I loved very much. One day, I wondered if it was possible to somehow sculpt his handsome features. Having never sculpted anything, with high hopes, I visited an art store and purchased some clay. From memory, with no picture to guide me, I molded a life-size bust of his head and neck. When you love someone, you know how that face and neck feel when you caress them. Our hands have a wondrous memory of their own.

The orangey clay color of the bust didn't seem very masculine, so later that week, I purchased some black paint and brushed it over the entire sculpture. When finished, the work was placed on the kitchen table in my apartment, draped with a towel. When my friend came over for a visit, I mentioned there was a surprise waiting in the kitchen. With a dramatic "Voila!" I whisked off the towel.

Astonished, he gasped, "Oh my gosh, it's *me!*"

It's my hope each reader will search his or her own life for innate talents that have come inexplicably, seeming not to be the result of genetic lineage.

Where do they come from? Who *knows?* Peoples' natural talents might be a powerful argument for reincarnation, the belief in past lives that is embraced by a majority of people around the world. Others, rejecting this concept, might insist these talents are random, just "the luck of the draw." Still other people might consider them one-time gifts from God. Whatever the answer, inborn talents remain one of life's beautiful *mysteries*.

College dorm mate studying
(sketched with her permission)

117

Still life, when home-made dripped bottles were all the rage in the 60s

Still life. The professor asked us to sketch whatever we could find.

Ink drawing from museum exhibit of "Napoleon On Horseback," by Henri de Toulouse-Lautrec
(I felt that the figures to the left and right were most interesting, and the most complex).

ALL ALONE

Do you remember a time when you felt profoundly alone? For me, such a feeling washes over my soul whenever a bee lights on my windshield at a stoplight.

"Oh honey, you are lost, and likely will never find your way home again. You are out in the world, adrift from those with whom you feel most at ease…the ones who understand who you are…the ones with whom you share a sense of purpose in your daily endeavors…the ones who keep you warm when the world outside is cold."

Some folks might consider this little insect an annoyance, and quickly flip on their windshield wipers to get rid of it. It isn't much help to the little one, but my choice is to remain quietly stopped until the light changes. Maybe the bee gets a small bit of comfort from the whirring vibration of the engine, even though it hardly mimics the familiar buzzing of its own kind.

As the light changes, I attempt to start up very slowly, gradually increasing speed. After the bee has flown away, my thoughts remain with it…offering blessings in its search for home and family.

Everyone has his or her own definition of what constitutes *loneliness*. It is often said families are groups of people into which we are born. Some systems of belief say we choose *which* family we wish to be born into, so that we may learn certain valuable lessons about life on earth. Regardless of our beliefs about birth families or adopted families, one thing is true for all of us: Friends are families we *choose*. Wherever we feel most comfortable becomes the *home* of our heart.

This is not an easy world. There are challenges at every turn. There are also moments of delight around many corners. We each need a gentle smile, even if it's from a stranger—and we each can be the stranger softening the journey of another. May gentleness surround each of us in every circumstance, no matter *where* the winds of life may lead.

JMcK

On St. Patrick's Day, March 17, 2010, my beloved Carol's brother passed away suddenly. His name was John McKievick. He had enjoyed a lifetime of success in the construction industry. John left no specific instructions about what to do with his ashes, or whether he would like to have a memorial service.

To honor John, four of us decided to go out to lunch, and offer a toast in his memory. We met at the Bombay restaurant in the Hillcrest area of San Diego. It's a beautiful place, complete with a floor-to-ceiling waterfall, and was voted the best Indian restaurant in the county.

Our luncheon party included Tom (John's older brother), Jim, a good friend, and Daisy, Jim's friend from Oklahoma. We enjoyed a wonderful lunch and raised our glasses to John. Daisy mentioned, during our conversations, that she really did wish to believe our lives go on after we pass away, but that she still remained a bit skeptical.

We all journeyed outside to say goodbye. Hugs were exchanged, and I got into my car parked out front. I was just getting ready to pull away, when someone tapped on the driver's side window. It was Jim.

"Jannie, come quick! You've got to *see* this!"

I followed him about twenty steps. There, in front of the restaurant next to the Bombay, carved in the concrete, were the initials *JMcK*. They were obviously a remnant from an earlier time, when the cement had been freshly poured.

As the three were walking back to their car, Tom had spotted the initials. How many of us, just strolling along, would be looking down at a sidewalk with enough awareness to notice initials left in the concrete? It was John's *brother*, not the two friends, whose eyes were drawn to that spot.

It seemed quite a miracle, given the hundreds and hundreds of wonderful restaurants in San Diego County. Upon arriving home, just out of curiosity, I opened the phone book's white pages filled with residential listings. Of 755 pages, only a little more than one side of a single page listed last names with the initials McK (McKewon, McKinney, etc.). If one looked under each name, thirty or more people might be listed. There are not many "McK" names. To top it off, the initial J was there. JMcK. John's initials were right there in front of us.

As I mentioned later to Tom, someday when we've all crossed over, we'll have to ask John for an explanation. Won't it be fun if he reveals that when he was younger, he knew the cement was fresh, and did the deed himself?

Such a story would be the icing on the cake of this particular miracle. Here's to you, John... We raise our glasses *high!*

THE BEE GEES

In the early part of 2010, I met a woman who was new to a class I'd been attending for years. She shared interesting news. She had the gift of channeling people who had crossed over. Noting the curiosity in my eyes, she cautioned, "It's not like a half-hour reading or anything. Usually, I just get a few sentences that I jot down on paper."

My loved one, Carol, had passed away in 1998. I asked if she might meditate on Carol's name. She said, "Sure," and promised to give the slip of paper to me in class the following Tuesday morning. Sunday was Valentine's Day. True to her word, on Tuesday, she gave me a note containing seven very special sentences. They sounded like something Carol would say, filled with love and heartfelt encouragement.

The woman related that, while she was meditating, she saw beautiful shades of red, ranging from dark to bright. Later, she told me they seemed like "globes of light." I associated the red with Valentine's Day.

At the bottom of her note, the woman had written, "I asked Carol to touch you, or give you a sign."

I was up late that night and didn't go to bed until 1:00 a.m. To reap the benefits of a good eight and a half hours of sleep, I set my clock radio for 9:30 a.m.

I awoke at 7:30 a.m. with a song in my head. It was the Bee Gees singing *How Deep Is Your Love?* from 1977. That particular song never had special meaning for me. It was just part of the hit parade of the time. It played over and over in my mind, and I wondered, "What is *this* all about?" It would not cease, but just kept repeating. Oh, well. I turned over and went back to sleep.

My clock radio clicked on at 9:30. The Bee Gees were singing *How Deep Is Your Love?* A miracle? You bet. I took it as the *sign* my new friend had requested from Carol. Later, I looked up the lyrics on *Google*. They are quite lovely, and do sound like something Carol would say.

For the wonderful beauty of the words, I say, thank you, Carol! Thank you, Universe! Another miracle to celebrate; one that brings a warm feeling of sweet surprise with each and every recollection.

Postscript July 6, 2010:

A few weeks ago, one of our San Diego radio stations (105.7 FM, "The Walrus") played *You're The First, The Last, My Everything* by Barry White, singing in his beautiful basso profundo voice. That song also never had a special meaning in my life. Yet, on this occasion, there were goose bumps all over my body. Through years of experience, I have learned to take notice when goose bumps happen, especially when the weather and air in the room are warm and comfortable. It usually comes from spirit, and means simply, *pay attention.*

This morning, my clock radio woke me with the above-mentioned Barry White song followed by *How Deep Is Your Love?* by the Bee Gees! *Both* songs occurred during the moments from 9:00 to 9:10 a.m.

In the deepest part of my heart, I do believe it is your love, Carol, initiating these synchronistic occurrences and goose bumps as time goes by. You were a generous and loving person while here on earth. It feels right to affirm once more the promise I made just moments before you passed: *I will love you forever and ever...and beyond.*

II. LYRICAL THOUGHTS
(Poems)

ON HOLDING MY DAUGHTER FOR THE VERY FIRST TIME

What will you be
And who will you know
As into this wonderful
Wide world you go

I wish you bright rainbows
And many a song
And nothing but smiles
Your whole lifetime long

It must be like heaven
This moment we share
I wish I could save it
Like a lock of your hair

It will pass as it must
This moment in time
But even as now
While I'm penning this rhyme

I will keep it forever
Where no one can see
Deep in the soul
Of the eternal "me"

Love's gift to the world
You have made it so much better
I just had to tell you
To write you this letter

God bless you and keep you
My dear little one
And I'll hold you and love you
Even after life's done—

Mama

FRIEND

Let me friend you
And mother you
But let me try not
To smother you

Let me laugh you
And cry you
Let me overcome
The shy you

Let me listen you
And hear you
Let me rest awhile
The weary you

Let me walk you
And talk you
And break apart
The rock of you

Let me sing you
And tease you
But always, always
Please you

Let me smile you
And thank you
For you're like me
Who loves what's true

And do I cherish you?
Are you blind?
The answer's YES
Dear friend of mine.

Related writing: "HONORING CAROL"

HOW CAN I TELL YOU?

How can I tell you…

Of loneliness no longer here
Of happiness more complete than I ever thought possible
Of hours spent thinking of you and the joy that activity
brings to my heart
Of the warmth that courses through me when we are
next to one another…and the way that warmth fills up
every "empty space" within me
Of how slowly the hours pass until next we meet
Of how I look at other people of late and feel regret they
can never know this happiness divine because
they don't love *you!*
Of what a treat it is to gaze into your face during
conversation
Of how your voice is the one I know which speaks
directly to my heart
Of your eyes which rummage around in the most private
rooms of my soul…and find warm welcome there

Even if you leave tomorrow, you have already given me enough
to fill up a lifetime of remembering the warmth of all of this.
THANK YOU.

In love forever,

Jannie

Originally written in pen to my beloved Carol in 1991, the above was rediscovered in December 2008. If you have ever been in love, perhaps these feelings will strike a chord in your own heart. My daughter Wendy thinks many people, whether gay or straight, will be able to identify. Why publish something so personal? We were closeted at a time when it was not possible to walk in the sun hand in hand and declare love openly. In 2011, it feels right. Love is love. Poets Robert and Elizabeth Barrett Browning openly expressed their love to the world. Ours is a love between two devoted people. Anyone in such a magnificent state of bliss can smile and agree with the familiar song, *Love is a Many-Splendored Thing!*

ELDERLY

This person who sits in a chair with wheels
Staring deeply into space
Who seems to care nothing for the world all around
If you judge by the look on his face

Was there ever a pair of baby shoes
That held his wrinkly old feet
Or a mischievous look in these now vacant eyes
When he stole from his mama a treat

Was there a tree rope hangin' over a pond
Where he swung and laughed a-splashin'
And maybe a dear one he loved
With what seemed *unlimited* passion

Did he once hold his baby and see in that face
All the promise of joy in his life
Did he sit at the end of a work-weary day
And softly confide in his wife

Stop! Don't pass by
Don't leave him alone
Just because he's no longer "new"
Look under the wrinkles
In back of the eyes

This person is me…and you

BLUE BEADS
(On coming out as gay in mid-life)

A red beaded bracelet
Adorned each little girl child
Upon arrival in this world
A place both gentle and wild

Sometimes one was chosen
Whose bracelet wasn't the same
One blue bead in the middle
Set her apart when she came

But things can be "fixed"
And as she grew
She learned to paint
She covered the blue bead in red
Making it something it "ain't"

All through life she played a role
Became just like the others
Did what the red-beaded ladies did
Even becoming a mother
(and loving it!)

But midlife rolled around
When people like to review
Their lives and their direction
To find an "honesty" brand new

She gazed at her little bracelet
There since the day she was born
The blue bead with paint peeling
Was looking sadly forlorn

"Time for a new coat," she sighed
"From the old bucket of red"
But then upon glimpsing
Her mirrored image
Across the room, above the bed

She smiled softly, "Not this time,"
And used some turpentine instead.

ON BEEING

Does he see this tiny bee
What I while watching him can see
If he doesn't
Oh how dreary
Just to be a little bee

The turmoil of his circling
All around the rosy bush
While all else all about him
Remains in silent hush

The stillness and the beauty
Are not seen by him I'm told
But merely the *usable essence*
Of the flower that he holds

It's but a matter of mechanics
Gathering from each tasty bud
Pollen here and pollen there
No more exciting than the thud
Of a hammer on a nail
Over when he's had his fill
And moves onward in his journey
To a bush atop the hill

Did he ever see the colors
Did he ever smell the smell
Before leaving each lovely scene
And scurrying quickly on pell-mell
To the next part of his life
That seems like the one before
It's amazing how the bee
Can keep from feeling like a bore

I wish that the bee could see
And, oh, that we all could *BE*.

MAY YOUR SWEETEST JOYS BE FOUND
IN THE SOFT WHERE OF LIFE

WHERE:

Morning bids you welcome with its sweet aroma of warm coffee
Your senses enjoy the first succulent bite of a perfectly ripened peach
You savor the delicate scent and soft texture of a rose laden with dew
Rain announces its rhythmic presence against a glassy pane:
Each drop meanders down the window, merges with its neighbor,
then randomly resumes its journey
Footsteps tread ever so gently upon crackling autumn leaves
Nature's tiny streams tumble over rocks, ending in a gurgling waterfall
You eavesdrop on chattering leaves shaken by a breeze in tree
branches overhead
Your fingers find a warm loving home in the soft fur of a devoted pet
Each color in a rainbow melts softly into the pastel band next door
A kite climbs and dips in an azure blue, marshmallow-puffed sky
Glistening white hills and valleys bear witness to newly fallen snow
Tumbling snowflakes make a "silent" sound as they settle upon the
shimmering white blanket covering hills and fields
You sway softly with your love to a rhythmic slow, slow dance
Daylight melts into twilight evening as you watch the night fall
The mellow sweetness of hot cocoa gives an assurance that "all is well"
Your ears delight in the bubbly giggles of children's laughter
Your lips tenderly brush the soft downy head of your newborn child
A snowy seagull with wings extended soars above in effortless flight
Pelicans glide in "V" formation above the reach of ocean waves

Bird songs outside your window are joined by the incessant whirring of
hummingbird wings
The gentle murmur of moonlit surf blends with the crackle of a toasty
campfire at the beach
Warm flames dancing in a fireplace give serenity to mind and heart
You snuggle into the warm quilted security of your very own bed
Your senses capture the soft breathing of your love lying beside you in
the purple light just before dawn

AND

You realize *LOVE* is the sweetest joy in life—the soft *where* you will
always be....

STREET PEOPLE

Be kind
Share
Think of me

Love
Care
Honestly

Touch
Feel
Open your heart

Smile
Give
At least
Make a start

To build of the world
A gentler place
Where love wears
A smiling face

Where sorrow
And cruelty
Are never at home
No one's forgotten
…No one's alone

A pipe dream they say
What can one person do
Maybe not much
But if we become two
Two leads to three
And then beckons to four
And after awhile
We've become so much more

We're a world all complete
A gentler place
Where love wears
A smiling face
Where sorrow
And cruelty
Are never at home

No one's forgotten and

…No one's alone.

LOVE
(Of the romantic kind)

Eyes that care
Smiles that share
Hands that caress with such gentleness
Lips that share feelings deep in the soul
Minds that understand and excite
Passions that know the joy of release
Sunsets that glow with
Promises of evening and dawning
Laughter that bubbles
Bright conversation
Movies to inspire and delight
Mutual regard for deeply felt emotions
Music that moves both body and soul
Long silences without need for words
Comfort in those silences
Scrumptious meals that nourish our bodies
While we fill each other's eyes with love
Long walks through nature
Long talks through days, nights,
Twilights and noontimes
Lingering looks
Filled with affection and love
Two hearts melded into one
Sharing always and forever
Tenderness.

FOR THE BIRDS

I never expected to find life's secret of contentment
on my trip to the beach that day.
But I think I did.

Two quite ordinary-looking little birds
perched atop a warm, sunlit rock,
sitting not half an inch apart, feathers puffed.

Every few seconds, one would lean toward the head of the other
and nuzzle briefly.
Then, they would return to sitting quietly next to each other,
watching the world go by.

Either could fly away at any moment, but neither wanted to.
Contentment lay in staying close to one another.
Happiness nestled in the sharing of each other's company.

Today, we all seem to be searching, searching, searching:
So busy with our exercising, looking good, making more money,
Proving our worth to heaven only knows who.

The birds know better.
To be happy, *most* of what we really need is simple:
Someone to *nuzzle*, to *share*...
and to *understand*.

FRIENDSHIP

Two vibrant leaves

Of deepest green

Always alive

Side by side

Floating together

On the winds of life

Feelings never to wither

Never to die

III. LIFE'S LESSONS LEARNED
(Essays)

JOY OF HEAVEN 24/7

Through the years, my life has been enriched by an assortment of experiences. Finally, as often happens in one's senior moments of reflection, I *get it,* and believe I know for certain the secret of happiness. That may sound pompous, but it does feel *true.* After a life of ups and downs, straight ahead successes, sideways turns, great joys and depths of sadness, at last everything has coalesced into a big bright light of *TRUTH.*

It seems so very simple. In every moment, if we walk gently in the world, hold fast to personal integrity, use our natural talents, respect the feelings of others, and act with compassion toward other people, animals, and Mother Earth—It doesn't matter *what* difficult challenge we face at any particular time. Deep joy is constantly present, if we but look for it. It always comes, as surely as springtime follows winter.

This is not the *giddy* kind of happiness that depends upon present circumstances in our lives. It's a deep, *deep* joy way down in the core of us, stemming from the realization of *who* we are: children of the Creator of All, able to feel confident, happy, and always moving forward in loving kindness, regardless of the events surrounding us. We don't *pursue* happiness, but rather *experience* it in every moment. We find something of value, even in the death of a loved one, disability, disease or whatever. Something beautiful can be found in every experience, whether it be a lesson learned, or blessings discovered in what remains—memories, the love and caring of family and friends, and any number of other special joys that exist all around us, if we but open our eyes to *see..*

There is another component to this surety of truth…stillness. Try finding a quiet moment in which all is still around you. Perhaps soft, wordless music is playing in the background. Sit or lie down with no one else around. Take three or four deep breaths and let them go. Clear your mind of thoughts. Do you *feel* it? It is a sense way down deep within that you are not alone. *Something* fills up your insides. It feels like a very soft buzzing vibration. It is the Life Force. This very real something fills your mind with calm assuredness. You can *relax.* In this state, and even in the busyness of life, there is a Presence that loves you. Call it whatever you wish. I call it Father/Mother Creator of All. Native Americans call it Great Spirit. Some people call it the Force, and some call it God. I tried to find the origin of that word on *Google.* There were so many different theories that I gave up. This Presence is the One who created you. It is your Parent. It is the One who has always been there in the hard times, when you had lessons to learn, and has rejoiced in all your good times. It never stops caring. It never leaves you.

Scientists tell us a *common energy* is found in and around every atom in the universe. Our entire universe is made up of this same *stuff*. When we look at the structure and order of all that exists, it seems logical that the Creator who brought everything into being has intelligence. People through the ages have noticed the grand design of small things (like snowflakes), as well as heavy round spheres like the earth and moon, which remain in predictable orbits year after year after year. At any moment, there are trillions of activities going on within each of us at the cellular level, without our conscious direction. The Life Force is making these happen, taking care of our bodies while we focus our minds on other things.

Science also tells us that all the cells of the body pick up on our mood and resonate to positive feelings. Years ago, *Time* magazine published an article noting that if a person smiles for even fifteen seconds (regardless of the way he or she is feeling), the body releases endorphins which are natural pain relievers. The person feels *better*. The power of a smile, to one who *receives* it, and the one who *gives* it, can never be overestimated.

Each of us is like a drop in the Ocean of All That Is. We can try to deny it if we wish, but is it easy for a drop of water to leap out of the ocean? We might as well relax, and swim in the wonder of it. God is in us, as well as all around us, in everything and everyone. We are a part of the Ultimate Wholeness of All, and, miracle of miracles, this Creative Father/Mother loves each of us as if there were only one of us. We need fear *nothing*, because of the Constant Presence which never leaves. It keeps the essence of each of us, our Spirit, *safe*.

We can give thanks to That Which We Do Not See. Our inability to see with our eyes does not mean the Force does not exist in the next dimension beyond our physical world. We each have been gifted by our Creator with individual talents that can be used to uplift others and better our world. We are able to follow our own bliss, exercising free will in all of our choices.

This Loving Force, the Ultimate, is also in every single one of our neighbors, no matter who they are. There is some good in the worst of us, and some bad in the best of us. Joy enters our lives when we recognize the core of All Goodness in every other person on earth. We all have the same Mother/Father Creator (Parent). When there is conflict, human beings are attacking a part of the Entire Being, which includes them *and* their foes. We are, in essence, attacking part of All We Belong To—a portion of our own Being. What kind of lunacy is that? How wonderful it would be if this basic understanding could come to those who espouse hatred, conflict and war, whether at the family or global level. What good does hurtful behavior accomplish? What benefit does it bring?

One can still be a realist. Yes, there are negatives in the world, and people who do try to harm others. It is necessary to defend those we love against cruelty in such situations. Happiness lies in being one of the *positive* people, working to help, not hurt, always looking up, not down. We can let go of our ego, which seeks recognition and validation from other people. Instead, we can feel fulfilled being part of the One, the Ultimate Good—able to look in the mirror and feel we have given our best effort in life. We find the Beauty of All also in animals, flowers, sunsets, ocean waves, mountains, rivers, and more. It can be seen in all of nature, which The Great Inventor created. This Mother Earth which sustains us deserves our profound respect. She is the magnificent *Home* provided for us, a *gift* from the One Who Loves Us Unconditionally.

Since my twenties, I've read countless stories of people who've traveled outside their bodies during "deaths" on the operating table. Later, they were resuscitated, and were able to recount their experiences. Renowned actress Jane Seymour told this story in a television interview some years ago: When she was younger, her heart stopped during an operation. Suddenly, she found herself hovering up in one corner of the operating room, watching the doctors below trying to save her life. She recalled being embraced by warm light and love, and feeling wonderful. Soon, she was drawn quickly back into her body at the moment of resuscitation. She experienced a new awareness that the only things we take with us when we cross over are our intelligence, feelings, the love we have given, and the love we have received. She made a commitment from that point on not to waste a single moment of the remainder of her earthly life on actions not born of, or having to do with, love. Today, she is an accomplished wife, mother, painter, and designer, in addition to being a talented actress.

In another story, after an operation (in which she clinically died for a time), a young girl mentioned that she had traveled outside the hospital. No one believed her until she described an old tennis shoe on a ledge outside a large window near her room. Curious, hospital personnel searched the ledge. They found the shoe, but it was in an area of the ledge not visible to someone looking through the glass from inside the hospital. It could only be seen from outside.

Some neuroscientists believe that our thoughts originate outside our physical bodies, outside the flesh of our brains. It's all a mystery, whether thought begins in our aura (the outer energy emanating from our bodies, which scientists have photographed), our soul (energy larger than our bodies alone contain), Universal Mind (all thoughts ever expressed), or multitudes of other possibilities. One theory put forth is that thoughts may enter our brains in the same way radio waves enter a television set. These thoughts are then organized within the brain, transmitted through speech, and thus communicated to others. Some of my own poetry came inspired from somewhere, and was written down on paper within five minutes.

Where does *inspiration* come from? Who knows? A wonderful example of someone inspired was Wolfgang Amadeus Mozart, who would write his compositions in ink. Virtually nothing needed to be altered from his original text. When one looks at other composers' work, notations are often crossed out and changed multiple times. Mozart's seemed to come to him already perfected.

As often as we wish to each day, we can talk to our Parent. We can talk to our Best Friend. We are never alone. We can confide our biggest dreams and deepest problems to One Who Cares, One Who Loves Us, One Who Made Us, and will be welcoming us *Home* again, once we have left these bodies of flesh. Science says energy can never be destroyed. Our souls (our energies) merely move on, intact. We will just be stepping into a different dimension of the Ocean. It will be like removing this overcoat of flesh and taking a step into Paradise…easy. That moment of transition will be our Ultimate Gift from the Father/Mother Creator of All, who loves each of us more than anyone else ever could.

These are my own beliefs about the secret of contentment: Relax in *all* of life, walk with kindness and compassion in every moment, laugh a lot, and smile often, knowing that the Greatest of All Beings holds us in the palm of His/Her hand and will keep us safe, *always*.

The Ultimate loves to shower us with good. It is both a nice idea and a privilege for us to say *THANK YOU,* and say it often, with sincerity. Whether we appreciate life's blessings and utter prayers of gratitude, or fail to do so, the good just keeps on coming, forever and ever… *without end.*

Related writings: "GOLDEN MOMENTS" and "MELTING"

GOLDEN MOMENTS

They come to us like precious coins, these moments of our lives:

1,440 per day…525,600 in a year…over 40,000,000 in an 80-year lifespan. We are each given them as a *gift* when we are born; precious coins of worth to put in our pocket and spend as we wish, day by day.

There are so many, perhaps at times we lose sight of how *valuable* each minute is; each a tick of the clock spent, *never to come again.*

The *coins* of a single life: What will they matter, once they have been spent, 100 or 1,000 years from now? Those well invested will mean a great deal, depending upon how each of us chooses to spend them.

Our choices come along every day. What will ultimately last and live on forever and uplift the whole human race depends upon our understanding of what might be called, "The Paradox of Permanence."

The Paradox is: What appear *indestructible* are the dense, material things of earth; diamonds and steel. They are what would seem to be the most permanent. But these and like substances eventually degrade and crumble. What lasts for all time are the *intangibles*, those things born of the noblest intention, *love.*

We can choose in each moment where to invest our coin. Some of our choices are between gratitude and indifference, best effort or mediocrity, compassion or contempt, truth or dishonesty, respect for the lives of others, or careless disregard, healthy skepticism or stubborn cynicism, quiet reflection or noisy "busyness," the fulfilling or the mundane, courage or cowardice, kindness or cruelty, optimism or pessimism, peace or disharmony.

How we invest each moment depends upon our focus, positive or negative. When confronted with the difficult, and the tragic, it helps to realize that in the whole of the earth, at that very instant, a mixture exists. At the moment one person dies, others are being born. In our circumstance may be a tragedy, but elsewhere someone is sharing time with a child, being a friend, comforting the sick, laughing, cutting a wedding cake, swimming in a coral reef, sharing romantic love, counting the stars, singing a song, petting a dog, or savoring a sunset.

By focusing and choosing with every tick of the clock, we each deposit another precious coin. All the coins ultimately comprise the *worth* of a single life.

We fine tune through the lens of our personal focus by refining our perspective every day, with another turn of our telescopic lens at each encounter. Our perspective is shaped for each of us in differing measure, depending upon our surroundings, our upbringing, our station in life, our education or lack thereof, our powers of discernment—and also by observing the behavior of those we admire and respect, and those we do not.

Each of us making an effort to understand the perspective of another will make for a more peaceful world. There is room in our world for diversity, whether we live in the material pomp of a Caesar or the poverty of a beggar—whether we possess the wisdom of a saint or the intolerance of a bigot. There is room for us all. The key is to communicate with one another without rancor, choosing to strive for mutual understanding.

We reap the benefit or pay the price for how we choose to invest our precious, irreplaceable coins. We are each responsible for our choices. Sometimes we are recognized and validated by others. At other times we may wind up behind prison bars, or pay the ultimate price for wrong choices that violate societal standards.

Tick, tock…A moment is gone. Then another coin presents itself. Our chance to begin anew! We have the opportunity to better our choices from the ones we have made in the past—to choose the wise, the positive, the courageous, the tender, the happy, and the most compassionate.

Intangibles, those things born of the noblest intentions, survive. Buildings and weapons disintegrate. Ideals and resolve remain. What about military strength and power? All tyrants eventually fall, and democracies endure, because free societies allow human hearts and spirits to be authentic and expand to their fullest potential.

Free people will always fight to preserve liberty, to keep it alive. Most of what endures *forever* of the human experience are thoughts and intentions born of *love,* the noblest attribute of humankind: compassion, empathy, tenderness, fairness, holding fast to noble ideas, and finding joy in doing our best and being authentic.

Every moment is a present to open, filled with limitless possibilities to uplift or diminish the ultimate human condition. A lifetime of all these possibilities *coalesced* matters very much indeed, and is of *infinite worth.*

When we each experience the last tick of the clock, hopefully we will have wisely invested our treasure, these golden moments, these coins of worth—melting them down into golden imperishable threads woven into the tapestry of humanity to make it more beautiful, to make it strong…comprised of the wealth of all of our shining moments.

Future generations may not remember our names, yet they will still inherit a positive legacy, one which is important: love, light, creativity, caring and compassion, strengthening the family connection of all humanity; our *moment* in the uplifting of all mankind, of all the earth and all that *is.*

MELTING

On June 15, 2009, I received a lovely long letter from a friend in Arizona. She described at one point the natural beauty she and her husband experienced during sunset and early morning:

"When we sit outside here in the evening and the air cools while the sky turns rosy and the hummingbirds flash past; and the quail perch on the wall announcing to the world that evening is nigh—or perhaps even more intense, the early morning—before the sun blazes above the mountain and we savor our coffee (mine) and cocoa (his) and the awaking birds—then all is right with the universe. The beginning and the ending balance anything that can come along in the day."

My friend then finished describing this place, "where one can melt into the greater being."

Upon reading that last sentence, suddenly all the truths I had ever experienced personally, read about, or heard in speeches from enlightened people, came tumbling together like pieces of a giant jigsaw puzzle. Or perhaps, using another analogy, singular dominoes standing on end, that with one light push, fall one after the other in quick succession. Boom! Everything made perfect sense in that one instant.

A woman who's spent decades studying the human brain at the National Institutes of Health (NIH) wrote that she had become convinced that thought originates *outside* the brain, and comes into the organic tissue as airwaves might enter a TV set. There, thoughts are processed and organized so one might communicate them to others through speech or writing. Could these thoughts originate in the Universal Mind (every thought which ever existed or will exist) or the human soul, which is bigger than our body?

Regarding the story of creation versus the theory of evolution: Could not *one day* to the Creator of All be equivalent to tens of thousands of earthly years? Isn't it possible both theories are correct and complement one another?

People of faith say that human beings are "children of God." Science in quantum physics says there is a common electrical *energy* that surrounds atoms of *everything* in the universe. This common energy is around the atoms of a rock, the bright eyes of a newborn baby, the feathers on the wings of a bird, the petals of a blooming flower, etc. This energy permeates *everything* in existence. Is it such a stretch to infuse that Creative Energy with Intelligence and Love for Its own creations?

For me, this is the definition of what people call "God." It is *in* all things, *creates* all things, and *loves* all of Its creation. As children of God, with this energy in the cells of our being, we each possess the DNA of this amazing Creative Force. Each of us is as one drop in the big ocean of that which is "God." None of us can *ever* be separated from this energy, because It is *everywhere in the universe.*

I begin my own evening prayers with "Father/Mother Creator of All." This is followed immediately with thanks for the day just ended, and all the blessings of my life to that very moment. It feels so comfortable to dialog with Everything That Is. It feels right, as if Someone hears, is listening intently, and cares. Each one of us has our own special way of speaking from our heart about subjects we choose to discuss in prayerful silence or out loud. It just feels natural to "melt into the greater being," as my friend put it.

There are gradations of belief among the peoples of the world. There are many religions. We each may or may not belong to one of them. A person might not be religious, but all people are spiritual beings. We all have *souls*—and yes, there does come a moment when each of us breathes our last. Or so it would appear. But I've come to believe that what we call "death" is just a shedding of the flesh, a stepping into the next dimension, with our soul, thoughts, and feelings still intact, still very much *alive*. We live on with the vitality of our "Being" as real and alive as the Creator of All itself.

With this knowledge, why should one not find *joy* in every moment of life on earth? Knowing our essence will never die lets us meet physical and mental challenges here on earth with a hopeful attitude. Yes, catastrophes happen. It is not the catastrophe itself that is paramount. It is the *reaction* we have to tragedy that is most important. How do we meet it: with our noblest response, or by caving in and accepting defeat? Are we able to persevere and go on with an understanding of *why* something happened, discovering a positive in even the most negative of circumstances? If life is eternal, what shall we *fear*?

When one realizes we are all parts of the same living Being, it is easy to act with compassion and kindness toward one another, all living things, and Mother Earth. After all, we are each cells of the same Body. If another person or animal is hurting, it is a part of our Self that is injured. We reach out to try to heal and restore that part. There is no *other*. Everyone is related to us.

I met a woman once who expressed a similar perspective. It was only recently that I realized what she was saying. She said she looked upon the whole world as if she *were* the whole world. Upon seeing a homeless person, a movie star, a rose, a high school student, a dog, a bird, a sunset, a river or a mountaintop, she would say to herself, "Hmmm. Now, *that's* an interesting part of me!" She felt connected to all of life.

Conversely, I feel strongly that those emotions arising out of hatred, anger, and depression cause negativity, stress, and ill health. Why? They are the opposite of the Creative Loving One. They seek to destroy and tear down, rather than create and build up. On the other hand, great kindness, compassion and creativity come as naturally as breathing. They seem to fit in a universe as beautiful and orderly as ours.

The world is what it is. There are conflicts and stormy emotions all around. There are those who would tear down and criticize, seeking to somehow feel more justified than, and superior to others. But there are also people of light and joy, who wish to constructively uplift the human and environmental condition— who wish to nourish Mother Earth, and restore the beauty and purity of our natural home, this uniquely blessed planet.

Oh what a world we would have if each of us treated everyone and all that is with kindness—if we supported one another in creative and positive endeavors, which benefit all of our lives. What if we could all just *RELAX*, take some deep breaths, and step forward in our lives with *confidence?*

May we each *melt* into every day, knowing we are a part of All That Is. We always have been, and always will be, *forever and ever.*

Related writings: "JOY OF HEAVEN 24/7" and "GOLDEN MOMENTS."

WHIRLED PEAS

Some time ago, I spotted *Whirled Peas* on a bumper sticker. My initial reaction was a slight grin, in appreciation of the creative humor. Then reality set in. I wondered if true peace on earth would *ever* come to pass.

It is now 2011. Chaos and uncertainty threaten the planet. There is fear among many of folks different from themselves in ethnicity and religious belief. This fear foments frustration ("If only everyone could be just like ME!"). If not ameliorated, the frustration leads to anger, and sometimes even escalates into violence. People persecute or even kill those whom they perceive as *different.*

What if we instead tried to get to *know* others who are different from ourselves? *Why* is he or she different from me? What are that person's dreams for his or her own future? How can I *help* this one be all that he or she can be? How can we work *together* to uplift the planet, our common home?

We are in the age of the Internet. Facts, rumors, and untruths circle the globe within minutes, sometimes seconds. Before we have sifted through them to discover the real truth, people are in the media expressing, or even shouting opinions. Why do we not instead take time to settle down and use our logic? Why not wait perhaps half a day, until the facts can be determined, and *then* have our discussions?

Often, we seem to be guided by what science describes as the *reptilian* part of our brains. It encompasses the "fight or flight" phenomenon, knee-jerk reactions to perceived threats. As stated above, we fear, we get angry. We strike out, trying to eliminate the cause of our fear. We resort to spiteful words and violent actions. In personal one-on-one conversations, no one gets to be *understood* by the person holding an opposing view, because the other is concurrently forming a response in his or her own mind. Both parties walk away frustrated, failing to understand one another.

Whether someone is a young child, teenager, adult or senior citizen… the need is still the same. A person wishes to be listened to and understood. How much more constructive it is, after someone has spoken, to respond, "So what you are saying is…." It indicates the listener hears, and is really trying to understand what is said.

Consider the following: Billions of people around the world follow spiritual leaders. If all the most prominent ones (including Jesus, Muhammad, and the Buddha) were seated at a large round table, how would they treat one another? Would they bicker? Would they shout? Would they call each other names? Would they try to kill each other? *Or* would they listen with respect and thoughtful consideration, trying to reach a peaceful consensus or logical compromise?

In our current global society, we tend to lump people together by groups. We paint with broad brushes. It has been reported that the overwhelming majority of Muslims are peace-loving people. A tiny minority belongs to a terrorist fringe that has distorted Islamic beliefs, justifying violence to achieve their own ends. Many in the Western world now fear anyone who is Muslim.

Profiled on a recent newscast was a Muslim family, all American citizens who have peacefully lived, worked and worshipped in the United States for four generations. A little 10-year-old boy in that family is now afraid when his mother goes to the grocery store, because her head is covered, making it obvious she is Muslim.

Islamic prayer rooms have existed at the Pentagon (attacked on 9/11) and Walter Reed Army Medical Center, in Washington, D. C., for many years. There are American employees in both who practice their Muslim faith on a daily basis, while serving our government, and tending to those who are ill. In addition, there are soldiers wearing the uniform of the United States military who are of the Islamic faith. How must it make them feel, one wonders, to put their lives on the line to defend a Constitution which guarantees religious freedom to *all* American citizens?

We need to beware broad brushes. Many religions profess: "*HERE* is where the *TRUTH* is." Each individual needs to find a place that feeds his or her own soul. The world has *many* different religions—it's sort of like ice cream. There may be 31 or more flavors, but only One Maker of them all. Some people like strawberry, others prefer chocolate or vanilla. Each of us likes the *flavor* of whatever belief system feeds our spirit. Perhaps we can learn to respect those who like strawberry, and not insist they eat chocolate. Our Constitution lets us pick and choose with its guarantee of religious freedom.

The topic of prejudices and broad brushes begs us to remember classes of people discriminated against in the history of the United States: Native Americans, African Americans, Jews, Irish, Japanese, Italians, women (right to vote, equal pay), gay people...the list goes on and on. Individuals might prefer to be recognized for the worth they possess *inside*. These prejudices bring to mind lyrics of the song *You've Got to Be Carefully Taught*, from the 1950s musical *South Pacific*. This song speaks of how young children are brought up to hate and fear people who are different from themselves—people whose eyes are "oddly made," or people whose skin is a "different shade."

A friend once remarked, "There can *never* be peace in this world!" Another said, "Some people are just *born* evil!" I choose to differ. For ten years, it was a special privilege to work as a volunteer, holding one-, two- and three-pound infants in a hospital neonatal intensive care unit. The physical warmth of another helps these babies to thrive. I believe with all of my being that every person has an inner core of goodness. It's there at birth. What great progress could be achieved by nurturing that core, shielding it from cruelty, helping it grow, and encouraging the inborn talents of each child with education and caring. If we can instill a desire to help others (all of humanity), coupled with a love for the environment and its natural wonders, we might raise a future population who *can* bring peace to all the world.

Anne Frank, optimistic child of the Holocaust, said it best. "I still believe in the goodness of people. People are basically good inside."

Consider different societies of the world. Most of us are much more *alike* than we are different:

We have mothers and fathers.

We have children.

We have extended families.

We work to earn a living.

We value education.

We wish to be healthy.

We feel most comfortable when we are *not* in conflict, either within our families, or in the world.

We each have feelings that can be nurtured or hurt by others. These *feelings* are humanity's common denominator.

In our current world environment, racism persists, despite years of progress in a positive direction. When will we all eventually realize there is only *one* race...the *human* race? There is only *one family* of all humans *being*. Each of us is a *miracle walking*, given the trillions of activities happening in each body at every instant, without one's conscious direction. One may be driving a car, shopping for groceries, reading a book, or hugging a child. Yet these internal events continue to go on, day after day, year after year—with the physical biology, emotional feelings, intellectual intelligence, and unique talents all working together, blended into one singular life.

We are all *neighbors* on this big blue sphere, hurtling through space. What if we could see one another through the eyes of the Creator of us all? Would we listen, and try to *understand* each other, just as our Parent understands each one of us? Upon meeting someone we know, or even a stranger, would we ask out loud, "How is *your* day going?" Might that question instantly be followed by a silent one, "And how can *I* make it *better*?"

In times of natural disasters, people often ask, "How could God let this happen?" The Creator invented the laws of nature and the laws of physics. They are immutable, and work the same universally. These laws provide order because they always work the same. What if gravity sometimes brought things down to earth, and at other times lessened, causing things to float upward? Natural law brings us all stability.

The *order* in our universe is extraordinary. The One who created natural laws also gives us sunsets, rainbows, bird songs, flowers, snow-capped mountains, ocean waves, air to breathe and water to quench our thirst.

Sometimes we "get it." We rise to become our noblest selves. One example occurs during natural disasters. We see families with children in peril, and our hearts respond. We *help* others.

All ancient texts, of whatever religion, were written before the advent of advanced telescopes and microscopes. *Hubble* has let us venture millions of light years into the universe. Planet earth is unique. Where else do you see another blue planet with vast oceans that cleanse it, with a nourishing atmosphere, with plentiful inland waters and soil, all giving gestation to variant forms of abundant life? One species on this whirling sphere builds skyscrapers, sends rockets into space, and studies microbiology to help cure its own diseases. Many in the human species care for one another, and care for Mother Earth. There is a diversity of Creation here, the equal of which we have not seen in other solar systems. We are *unique!* It seems fitting to appreciate life, to nurture one another, and to respect the other forms of life dwelling here. Just *BEING ALIVE* is a miraculous experience!

People often speak about setting goals. Here's a worthy *ultimate* goal: To achieve peace on earth. With such a peaceful environment, each of us could happily strive to reach the best place our talents could lead us, without the distraction of hostility and chaos. Those talents could become our *career*. We would be compensated monetarily for doing what we love best. As the old saying goes, "If you love what you do, you'll never work a day in your life."

My neighbor Laura shared her own concept of how we might achieve world peace. She envisions a huge gathering of mothers. Some are mothers of babies. Others have lost children to wars and other violence. One group is in the throes of wonderful happiness. The other group suffers the turmoil of bitter tragedy. Would *ANY* of them be satisfied with a world as it exists today? Very quickly they would all agree with one basic axiom: No more war. Not *ever*. Peace could take root. Mothers who had lost children would wish violence had never existed. It took away those most precious to them. New mothers would abhor a future which would put their children in harm's way.

The United States was founded upon freedom of speech and religion. People can say and believe whatever they wish. If our country is torn apart because of hatred, prejudice, shouting, and violence against any form of religion, the terrorists (a tiny minority), by inciting fear and anger, will have triumphed. Current political shouting and rancor tear apart the fabric of our nation and our world.

Former British Prime Minister Tony Blair recently expressed in a television interview that religious cultures of extremism may pull the world apart in the 21st century. He said if we recognize the goodness at the core of every person, we might all strive instead to bring the world together, understanding one another, while condemning violence and war.

The choice is ours. We can heal ourselves and the earth peacefully, OR violently destroy the earth and all of society, leaving our world in chaos and destruction.

It all comes down to personal behavior. Picture two people, both waking up on the same morning: One thinks, "Today, I will act in kindness. At every moment, I will ask myself, 'Is this a kind thought, word or action?'" The other person asks, "Who can I insult, bully, gossip about, yell at, or physically injure today?"

Writer Maya Angelou shared the following: "I've learned that people will forget what you said, people will forget what you did, but people will never forget how you made them *feel*."

World peace hopefully begins with each individual heart and soul yearning to *be* good, which leads to *doing good*. Ultimately, these actions lead to *feeling good* about ourselves and others (low self-esteem often causes anti-social or even criminal behavior). Positive actions help us to be happy. If enough people *act positively*, it might finally lead to world peace.

"But I'm only one person," some will say. Many years ago, I read about the Power of One. Enough Ones all over the world living positive lives *could* bring about world peace. We can make a heaven on earth if enough of us dare to dream the *ULTIMATE DREAM*. Yes we can, if we *will*.

Singer Jimi Hendrix once expressed it this way: "When the power of love overcomes the love of power, the world will know peace."

This book has been all about miracles. I tried to follow where the persistent instinct of love (gut feelings) led me, honestly intending good for others, giving gratitude to Someone Greater. Every single experience is beneficial. If something is good intrinsically, it is good. If something is challenging, it is good because we learn a lesson from it. I've tried every day (and sometimes stumbled) to live positively. All this has led to deep joy way down in the core of my being. Such joy is not dependent upon exterior happenings. No one can take it away. Life keeps getting better and better as years go by.

The surprising synchronicities in this book remain a mystery. Each one led to a sense of wonder, "How did *that* happen?" I do not believe any of them happened "by chance." Perhaps when we each cross over one day, these fascinating miracles in our lives will be explained. *THANK YOU* to the Source of them.

Here's a parting thought, one constant goal toward which it's been fun to aspire:

"Be kind. Never fear. Only love."

Ever an optimist, I believe our *best* is yet to come. If enough of us in this world hold fast to living the ideal of peace in our daily lives, world peace might one day become a reality. Philosopher Norman Vincent Peale said it this way: "Hold an image of the life you want, and that image will become fact."

Since my first job was in Disneyland ("1963...THE MOUSE...AND ME"), it seemed fitting to close this book with a sentiment expressed in the song *A Dream is a Wish Your Heart Makes* from the Disney motion picture, *Cinderella.* The lyrics urge us to have faith in our dreams and someday...if we keep on believing, "The dream that you wish will come true."

With love and best wishes,
Jannie
P. S. Please always remember, you are never "alone."
No one is alone.

CPSIA information can be obtained
at www.ICGtesting.com
Printed in the USA
235933LV00001B